This *Spectred* ISLE

A footstep, a low throbbing in the walls,
   A noise of falling weights that never fell,
Weird whispers, bells that rang without a hand,
   Door-handles turn'd where none was at the door,
And bolted doors that open'd of themselves.

ALFRED, LORD TENNYSON, 'THE RING'

This *Spectred* ISLE

A JOURNEY THROUGH HAUNTED ENGLAND

SIMON MARSDEN

Words by Val Horsler & Susan Kelleher

ENGLISH HERITAGE

Published by English Heritage,
NMRC, Kemble Drive,
Swindon SN2 2GZ

www.english-heritage.org.uk

English Heritage is the
Government's statutory advisor
on all aspects of England's
historic environment.

Text © 2005, 2006
Val Horsler and Susan Kelleher
Photographs © 2005, 2006
Simon Marsden

www.simonmarsden.co.uk

First published 2005
ISBN-10 1 905624 17 4
ISBN-13 978 1 905624 17 1
Product code 51249

10 9 8 7 6 5 4 3 2 1

British Library Cataloguing in
Publication Data
A CIP catalogue record for this
book is available from the British
Library

Design by Andrew Barron,
thextension

Printed by Deckers Druk

Acknowledgements

Many of the stories in this book
come from English Heritage site
staff who responded some years
ago, and more recently, to
requests to contribute stories
about their sites. Some of them
have since left the organisation,
but the names of those we have
on record are listed here, with
grateful thanks for their help:
Duncan M Aitson; Mike Blair;
Daryl Burchmore; Yvette
Cannon; Jeremy J L Coles;
Hilary Doyle; Janet Giffin; June
Haines; Julie Hall; Mark Hartley;
John Heslop; Susan Howells;
Stanley Jenkins; David Lake;
Graham Lee; Sue Leech; Dave
Lofting; Vicky Martin; Clifford
Morris; Wendy Page; Ray
Phillips; Sheila Sayce; Ken Scott;
Dorothy Sewart; H A Smith;
Robert Snow; Sue Taviner;
Jennifer Waldron; Julie Wareing;
Antoinette Woollven; and
Phil Wyborn-Brown.
Margaret Wood did a sterling job
in collecting all the information
and ensuring that it was kept
securely filed.

The authors would like to thank
the following for their help
during the writing and
production of the book:
Polly Allison for research and
assistance in ordering the
material; Betty Beaty for her
inspirational ideas; Tamsin Gullen
for research and advice; Peter
Gunn for providing first-hand
knowledge of RAF sites; Liz Ives
for her invaluable research and
for the benefit of her extensive
knowledge of Yorkshire; Rob
Richardson for having the idea in
the first place; René Rodgers for
reading and commenting on the
draft text.

We are also indebted to
Gay Baldwin, author of
Most Haunted Island
(published October 2004),
for her permission to include
stories from her book about
ghosts at Osborne House on
the Isle of Wight.

Simon Marsden would like to
thank Sir Humphry Wakefield Bt,
of Chillingham Castle;
Lord and Lady Lytton Cobbold
of Knebworth House;
Gray Levett of Grays of
Westminster – exclusively Nikon
– for supplying photographic
equipment – and a special thank
you to Andrew Barron for his
inspirational design and undying
patience.

Many of the sites in this book
are in the care of English
Heritage. Entry is free for
English Heritage members.
For further details of opening
times and how to join,
please ring 0870 333 1181
or refer to our website:
www.english-heritage.org.uk

**Most of the places in this
book are properties in the
care of English Heritage,
but there are a few others
too, scattered through the
text and round the country.
We included some because
we liked the stories, others
because there was a
marvellous photograph and
yet others because they
bore some sort of relation
to an English Heritage
site close by. In addition,
where there were English
Heritage sites with
great stories but no
accompanying photographs,
we have sometimes
included them. The choices
have been personal ones,
for which we make no
apology.**

ILLUSTRATION ON PAGE 2
*Chillingham Castle,
Northumberland.*
ILLUSTRATION ON PAGE 5
*Statue at Toddington Manor,
Gloucestershire.*
ILLUSTRATION ON PAGES 6 & 7
*The graveyard at Whitby
Abbey, North Yorkshire.*
ILUSTRATION ON PAGE 8
*Detail from a tomb, Brompton
Cemetery, London.*

'Seeing the man she loved so happy in the company of his wife and children she turned away from the window and walked slowly through the yew walk into the park, her eyes downcast and wet with tears. Passing through the tall wrought iron gates she followed a winding path strewn with autumn leaves until before her, shrouded in mist, stood the great oak tree. Resting her back against it she reached beneath the folds of her dress for the knife and in one swift movement plunged it into her heart.'

I spent my childhood in two very haunted manor houses in the heart of the Lincolnshire Wolds, a remote area of the English countryside. My father kept a large library of books on the occult and in the long winter evenings would tell us four children ghost stories by the fire. The lines above are from his version of the tragic tale of *The Spanish Princess*, or *The Green Lady* who haunted the second of these mansions. In the drawing room hung an oil painting of this beautiful woman in a green dress who was to have a great and lasting effect on me. It was accepted by family and servants alike that her distraught spirit haunted the house, and I developed a real and lasting fear of ghosts – so much so that I sometimes wonder whether my lifelong obsession with photographing haunted sites is my way of trying to exorcise this fear.

My childhood belief in psychic phenomena has been enhanced over the years by many strange occurrences. Although many of these have been harmless, sometimes I have unwittingly placed myself in great danger, and experienced real fear in the presence of evil. While taking photographs for a previous book, *The Haunted Realm*, I was knocked flying by an unseen force near the Rollright Stones in Oxfordshire (see page 103–4). My camera was torn from around my neck and later that night I discovered a bruise the length of my arm that bizarrely did not hurt.

Two years ago, while making a film called *The Twilight Hour* in Ireland, the director, myself and other members of the crew all heard a terrifying cry for help inside an eerie ruin – not once but twice. None of us could explain this haunting plea, but will never forget the experience. Then last October I was invited by BBC Radio 4 to select the most haunted building I knew for a live radio programme. I chose Leap Castle, again in Ireland, and during the broadcast a ghostly voice mysteriously appeared on the programme and was heard by thousands of listeners. Again, nobody had a rational explanation. Sometimes I wonder whether it is my presence that activates these phenomena.

> *What may this mean,*
> *That thou dead corpse, again in complete steel,*
> *Revisits thus the glimpses of the moon,*
> *Making night hideous, and we fools of nature*
> *So horridly to shake our disposition*
> *With thoughts beyond the reaches of our souls?*

My 16-year-old daughter was recently studying Shakespeare's *Hamlet*, from which the above quotation comes, for an English exam. At the end of the first lesson her teacher asked if anyone in the class believed in ghosts? There was a silence and the students glanced round at each other to see if anyone would put up their hand. She was the only one. After the teacher left her classmates gathered round, telling her how brave she was to voice her belief, as they feared they would be ridiculed if they had done the same.

Fear rules our lives. Everything we do, or don't do, is in some way influenced by this powerful emotion. Perhaps this is why there are always people ready to ridicule those who genuinely respect the supernatural. How sad that we are unable to accept such honest beliefs that cannot be explained; why should there always be a rational explanation for everything? Is it really so surprising that we should share our world with the spirits of so many of our ancestors? We often behave as if we actually own space, but why can't we simply accept the existence of these ghosts and share it with them? Over the 30 years that I have been photographing haunted sites, probably 5–6,000 to date,

I have captured on film things that I can't explain. But it would be a fruitless task to try and prove to a disbelieving world that these photographs are genuine, and for this reason I keep many of these extraordinary images hidden.

When I was asked by English Heritage to do this book it was the perfect commission – revisiting my past, going back to my childhood among so many ancient and historic sites and the eerie tales of the ghosts that haunt them. For strange as it may seem, despite my fearful adolescence, it is among these sites that I feel most secure. We can't deny our past, although in an age when technology is the new religion, there are many who would have us believe it is irrelevant. The past has made its mark at all these locations and in our psyche too. It has made us who we are, and we can't deny the lives and deeds of the myriads who went before us.

Science and technology are often powerless in the face of nature and the supernatural. Witness the recent catastrophic events in the Far East where the horror of the tsunami destroyed so many lives. Remarkably, some 800 of the world's last true Stone Age tribesmen, who were at first thought to have been wiped out by the disaster, were later found to have survived intact along with their animals. They had taken to the high ground hours before the tidal waves struck, still in tune with their sixth sense and the hidden powers of nature.

I believe that another dimension – a spirit world – runs parallel to our own so-called real world and that sometimes, when the conditions are right, we can see into and become part of this supernatural domain. For me it is a question of how receptive we are willing to be, how far we are prepared to open our minds to this intermingling of physical and paranormal worlds. Walk through the creaking door of an old ruin and experience what science can never define – the overwhelming silence of our past. Here you are part of something far more tangible and evocative than the present, and as twilight descends feel the invisible shades of your ancestors watching you from within the dark passageways, a reminder of your own mortality.

Sir Simon Marsden
January 2005

The walls of Clifford's Tower bleed. Thomas, Earl of Lancaster, stalks his castle at Dunstanburgh, carrying the mangled head which Edward II's bungling executioner took eleven strokes to sever. The Rollright Stones possess a strange force that can fling you to the ground and leave you confused and uncertain where you are.

Cynics will say that it is the iron oxide in the stone used to build Clifford's Tower that flows red in the rain; and that the ruins of medieval castles and prehistoric stone circles are eerie enough in themselves on dusky winter evenings to evoke the shivers down the spine and the tingle at the back of the neck that conjure up ghosts and ghouls. But to psychic investigators, ghost hunters and those in search of something beyond the everyday and the humdrum, ghosts, spectres and things that go bump in the night are the evocation of the traumas of the past – events so momentous that they leave their imprint on the places where they happened.

People do see ghosts – even apparently level-headed people who dismiss such phenomena as tricks of the light or 'bound to have a perfectly natural explanation'. And the buildings of the past – particularly perhaps those that now lie ruined and abandoned – are rich in myths, legends and strange phenomena. Dismiss them as you may, rely all you will on the certainties of science, the anti-superstition of the modern world, but the unalterable fact is that these tales of the unknown are part – an essential part – of the story of the place.

Not all ghosts are frightening. Headless medieval lords are probably best avoided, as are spectral medieval ladies like Lady Howard at Okehampton Castle who is said to appear every night at midnight in a chariot made from the bones of her four dead husbands. But there is also the lovely lady in the frothy white dress at Beeston

Castle who appears only to children, smiling over her shoulder at them in broad daylight, unseen by adults and quite unalarming. Second World War personnel still go about their business in the tunnels at Dover Castle untroubled by modern visitors, and a cohort of Roman soldiers wades knee-deep through a cellar in York, marching purposefully along the Roman road still there half a metre under the modern floor level.

Historic places are imbued with legends too, and (possibly) true stories. It seems that Lord Scarsdale of Sutton Scarsdale Hall in Derbyshire was so appalled by the execution of King Charles I that he had his grave dug in the grounds of the Hall and went and lay in it every Friday to reflect on the sorry state of earthly affairs. The 'licking stones' in the dungeon at Carlisle Castle are said to have been worn away by the tongues of countless prisoners whose only means of easing their thirst was to suck at the moisture running down the walls. The body-shaped lead coffins still to be seen in the little chapel at Farleigh Hungerford Castle – among them presumably mothers who died in childbirth, entombed with the tiny coffins of their babies on top of them – were once real people with real lives. Who were they? What were their names? And why are their coffins still lying there in that small, semi-public place, after so many centuries?

Folk memories persist, even if the germ of truth at their heart becomes so overlain by later exaggeration and embroidery that it can never be disinterred. Is it possible that Joseph of Arimathea was a Jewish metal trader who brought his young kinsman, Jesus, to Cornwall on one of his trading trips? William Blake knew the story, and immortalised the idea in his hymn, 'Jerusalem'. More tangible perhaps is the possibility that the Cornish myth of Tristan and Isolde has its roots in a real Tristan who lived there; an ancient standing stone near Fowey is inscribed with the words *'Drustanus hic iacet Cunomori filius'* – 'Here lies Drustan, the son of Cunomorus'. There once really was a Drustan/Tristan.

Archaeological science tells us that of course the bluestones at Stonehenge were transported there from the Preseli Mountains in Wales; recent archaeological investigation near the monument uncovered a grave whose occupants came from that area. But isn't it much more romantic to imagine them flown there from Ireland through Merlin's magic powers? And aren't the brooding towers of Reculver far more menacing when they echo with the cries of a baby, sacrificed here by the Romans?

Some of these stories are real and tangible, others more smoky and mysterious. But whether you are a believer or a non-believer in legends and ghostly phenomena, a visit to an historic site is bound to be enhanced by the stories that cling to it. And this journey through English Heritage sites – and some other intriguing places near them – focuses on this 'other side' of the picture. Guidebooks will tell you about the architecture, the history, the people who lived and worked and died in these historic places. But here you will find the legends and the mysteries, the tales of the unexpected, the shivery unknown, and the fascinating stories that bring the places to life and clothe the ruins.

The stories are a journey, starting in the far south-west of England amidst the ancient landscapes of Cornwall, and ending in the north-east on the holy island of Lindisfarne. They are a journey in time too, from the unknowable mysteriousness of the prehistoric through to the ghosts of the Second World War and later. All kinds of sites are here, from tombs to Roman forts and medieval abbeys, and the castles that saw death and mayhem and are consequently the haunt of the headless and the frightening. Great houses too, some still roofed and furnished, some ruinous, have their share of tales. So, let us draw back the veil and meet the ghosts of this many-spectred isle.

OPPOSITE *The remains of a magnificent doorway at Old Wardour Castle, Wiltshire.*
PREVIOUS PAGE LEFT
Allerton Park, North Yorkshire.
PREVIOUS PAGE RIGHT
Sculpture, Toddington Manor, Gloucestershire.

THE SOUTH-WEST

And at midnight when the noon-heat breathes
    it back from walls and leads,
They've a way of whispering to me – fellow-wight
    who yet abide –
In the muted, measured note
Of a ripple under archways, or a lone cave's stillicide…

THOMAS HARDY, 'FRIENDS BEYOND'

St Michael's Mount

CORNWALL

This magical rocky island off the Cornish coast opposite Marazion is accessible by causeway at low tide and by ferry boat when high tide has cut it off from the mainland. It is dominated by its castle, built in the 14th century, but the origins of the Mount are said to go back to a giant, Cormoran, who wanted to build a home here raised above the trees so that he could keep watch on his neighbours. He preferred the white granite rocks to be found in the surrounding hills, but his wife, Cornellian, grew tired of travelling further and further afield to find them, so started to collect greenstones instead which she carried in her apron. Her husband, greatly displeased, kicked her hard, and the stones flew out of her apron and landed in the sand. One of them is still there, it is said, visible in the photograph above, immovable by any human power.

Cormoran was the terror of the country around, as he used to wade ashore and steal cattle and sheep from the fields on the mainland. One day a young boy rowed out to the island when the giant was asleep and dug a great hole. In the morning he stood beside the hole and blew a horn to wake Cormoran, who rushed out with the sun in his eyes and fell into the hole. The local people celebrated the lad who had slain the giant by calling him Jack the Giant-Killer and commemorating him in verse:

Here's the valiant Cornishman
Who slew the Giant Cormoran

The St Aubyn family have lived at St Michael's Mount since the 17th century, and have refurbished the castle and its gardens. There is a ghost too: a tall and confused figure that haunts the Priory Church. It may be the spectre of a

Chysauster Ancient Village

CORNWALL

tall man whose skeleton was found in the 19th century when renovation work in the church revealed a small dungeon reached by a stone stair. The entrance is now hidden by the family pews. But the well into which Cormoran was lured is still visible on the island.

This well-preserved Iron Age village was occupied from about 100 BC to AD 300. Its large, oval houses, with their open hearths, stone basins for grinding corn and covered drains, stand along what is recognised to be one of the oldest streets in the country. All the houses had terraced gardens, and the stone-walled fields belonging to the community are still to be seen outside the wall that encloses the village. There is also a fogou – one of the mysterious underground passages that occur in this part of Cornwall.

People came to Chysauster from miles around in the early 19th century to hear the preaching of Methodist ministers who used it as an open-air pulpit. And ghosts have been seen too – small men running round between the houses, thought to be the spirits of the village's original inhabitants.

PREVIOUS PAGE LEFT
Death mask of a member of the Hungerford family, Farleigh Hungerford Castle.

PREVIOUS PAGE RIGHT
Great Hound Tor, Dartmoor.

ABOVE *The remains of Chysauster Ancient Village, the haunt of spirits from our distant past.*

OPPOSITE *The mystical castle on St Michael's Mount.*

Tintagel Castle

CORNWALL

In an early example of shrewd marketing, the Cornish village of Trevena took advantage of the updating of the postal service in 1900 by renaming itself Tintagel, and thus put itself in an excellent position to exploit the explosion of interest during the 18th and 19th centuries in the Gothick past and the legends of King Arthur.

The early history of the site is shadowy, but at some point in the post-Roman era a wall of earth, stone and timber was built across the neck of the headland here, creating the stronghold that became known as Din Tagell. The medieval castle whose ruins can be seen today was built by Richard, Earl of Cornwall, in the 13th century. He may never have intended it to be a genuine stronghold: the north Cornish coast had little strategic importance, and the difficulties of building on the site were extreme. But

the legends of King Arthur, created in 1136 by Geoffrey of Monmouth in his *History of the Kings of Britain*, had their roots in Tintagel and, as a powerful force beyond Cornwall and England, and into Europe, there were major political gains to be made from the Arthurian link.

Arthur, king of the Britons, was said to have been born at Tintagel to the beautiful Igraine, wife of Duke Gorlois of Cornwall, and King Uther Pendragon, who through the wizard Merlin's sorcery was disguised as Gorlois and was thus able to enter Tintagel where Igraine was being kept in hiding. Arthur, the child they conceived, was put under the guardianship of Merlin, who later also devised the test that would reveal that Arthur was the true king when he alone was able to pull the sword from the stone. He became a powerful leader, and surrounded himself with the Knights of the Round Table who were great, chivalrous heroes. The stories of Sir Launcelot,

Sir Bors, Sir Galahad, Sir Perceval, Sir Gawaine and Sir Bedivere still resound. We still seek Camelot, the home of the Round Table and the fabled centre of Arthur's kingdom, where his queen, Guinevere, and Sir Launcelot conducted the doomed love affair that eventually led to the breaking of the fellowship of the Round Table and to Arthur's mortal wound at his last battle at Camlann.

Dozmary Pool nearby… the search for the Holy Grail… Glastonbury, reputed to be Avalon, burial place of Arthur and Guinevere…. the tale of Sir Gawaine and the Green Knight…. The legends surrounding Arthur all start at Tintagel.

Tristan and Isolde were also here. Tristan's uncle, King Mark, had his court at Tintagel, and sent his nephew to Ireland to bring the beautiful Isolde back to be his queen. But on their way back the pair drank a powerful potion that made them fall in love with each other forever. After Isolde and Mark married, the king found out about their love affair and forgave his wife but banished Tristan to Brittany where he met and married another Isolde but never forgot his true love. When he later fell ill he sent for Isolde from Tintagel in the hope that she could cure him.

He asked the ship's captain to hoist white sails on the return journey if Isolde was on board and black sails if she was not. Tristan's wife Isolde saw the ship approaching with white sails aloft, but lied to Tristan that they were black, whereupon he sickened and died.

It is easy, at Tintagel, to see why this place has legends swirling all round it. The coast is wild and rocky, the ruins of the castle seem to blend seamlessly with the natural landscape, the wind never dies down. To stand in Merlin's cave on the shore and watch the waves advancing inexorably is to feel a shiver of fear at the thought of being trapped here. And local legend has it that once a year the clouds roll back, the wind dies and the castle reappears in all its former glory – for a brief moment!

The grave of Excalibur

BODMIN MOOR

Dozmary Pool, near the infamous Jamaica Inn on the bleak expanse of Bodmin Moor, is the supposedly bottomless lake into which the dying Arthur ordered Sir Bedivere, one of the Knights of the Round Table, to hurl his famous sword, Excalibur. Twice Bedivere failed to throw the sword, and twice Arthur rebuked him. When, on his third attempt, Bedivere finally forced himself to hurl the sword into the pool, the arm of the Lady of the Lake emerged to catch it and hold it triumphantly aloft before disappearing with it for ever beneath the waters. And that is not the only legend associated with this haunting place. The spirit of a mystery man called Jan Tregeagle is here too, condemned after he murdered his wife and children to drain the pool using only a broken shell. A pack of ghostly wild dogs watches over him to prevent his escape… but others say that escape he did, to Porthcurno Cove where he sweeps the sand from the Cove to Mill Bay, only to be heard howling in anguish when the tide turns and the sea sweeps it all back again.

OPPOSITE *Tintagel Castle, the legendary birthplace of King Arthur.*
LEFT *Dozmary Pool on Bodmin Moor.*

OPPOSITE *Lydford Castle,*
haunted by the ghost of the
infamous Judge Jeffreys, known
as the 'Hanging Judge'.
RIGHT *The mysterious stone*
circles on Bodmin Moor
known as The Hurlers.

Hurlers Stone Circles

CORNWALL

The situation of these three large, aligned stone circles on moorland between the Rivers Fowey and Lynher would once have been an ideal meeting place for trade and community rituals. The stones all vary in shape but have been carefully erected so that they are the same height. One has a cleft in its top.

The legend surrounding them is the same as that of so many other stone circles: they are men turned to stone for breaking the Sabbath. In 1610 the antiquarian William Camden wrote of them: 'The neighbouring inhabitants terme them Hurlers, as being by devout and godly error perswaded that they had been men sometime transformed into stone for profaning the Lord's Day with hurling the ball.'

And again as usual with so many stone circles, if you do succeed in counting them accurately something nasty is likely to happen to you.

Lydford Castle

DEVON

On the western edge of Dartmoor stands Lydford Castle, a 12th-century tower once notorious as a prison and described during the reign of Henry VIII as 'one of the most heinous, contagious and detestable places within the realm'. It is reputed to be haunted by the ghost of Judge Jeffreys, known as the 'Hanging Judge' because of his ruthless pursuit of the defeated followers of the Duke of Monmouth after the Battle of Sedgemoor in 1685. Monmouth himself was executed at the Tower of London, where it took the executioner five strokes to cut his head from his body, but his captured soldiers were hanged in their scores all over the West Country by the merciless Judge.

There is another ghost here too – a black hound, said to be the spirit of the wicked Lady Howard, who also haunts Okehampton Castle nearby.

Kitty's Steps

DEVON

Water sprites or white ladies are to be found at many springs and waterfalls, enticing passers-by to join them in their watery homes. The beautiful Lydford Gorge has many waterfalls, including the tall, slender one known as 'The White Lady', and a smaller, more secluded one called 'Kitty's Steps'. The story goes that an old lady called Kitty was returning home through the gorge one evening, and as usual did not follow the path but took a short cut by this small waterfall. But that night she failed to return home, and it was not until several days later that her red headscarf was found near the pool. Her ghost is said to return to the spot on the anniversary of her death, staring into the dark waters of the pool with head bowed.

Okehampton Castle

DEVON

Every night at midnight Lady Mary Howard rides from her old home near Tavistock to Okehampton Castle in a coach made from the bones of her four dead husbands and with a skull on each corner of the roof. A headless coachman is her driver, and she is accompanied by a skeletal, one-eyed hound whose task it is to pick a single blade of grass in its mouth before they embark on the return journey. She is doomed to do this every night until the castle mound is picked clean of grass.

The real Lady Mary Howard, born in 1596, did indeed have four husbands who all died before her, and also had a magnificent coach built with four pineapples at the corners of the roof. She had become a considerable heiress after her father killed an innkeeper, and then himself, in a drunken rage, and was promptly married off, aged only 12, to her guardian's brother. She was

OPPOSITE *The waterfall in Lydford Gorge known as Kitty's Steps and the haunted pool below it.*
OVERLEAF *Okehampton Castle, where the ghost of the notorious Lady Mary Howard rides in her coach of bones.*

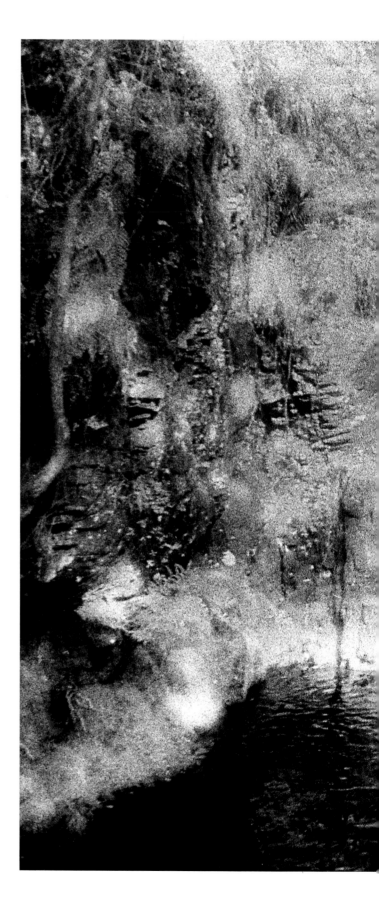

rumoured to have had a hand in the deaths of her husbands, but was almost certainly blameless. It may have been her insistence on ensuring that husband number four could not get his hands on her estate that led to her being regarded as suspicious and wicked.

Lady Mary was a member of the Courtney family who owned Okehampton Castle for much of its history. It was never besieged, but its importance lay in its symbolic and actual power at the centre of feudal and aristocratic dominance of society and land. Lady Howard is not its only ghost: a black hound can also be seen sometimes, whose glance is said to predict death within the year.

ABOVE *Great Hound Tor on Dartmoor where the strange rock formations are surrounded by tales of witchcraft and the Devil.*

Hound Tor Deserted Medieval Village and Great Hound Tor

DEVON

The deserted village here was originally settled in the Bronze Age and was occupied until the Middle Ages when it was abandoned. The area is riddled with legends and tales of mystery, no doubt rooted in the bleakness of Dartmoor and the strange geological shapes of the tors and the outcrops of rock that are so characteristic of this region, and which seem to assume a life of their own on dark winter evenings. The Devil figures large in these stories, reputedly stalking the area at night with his pack of wild hounds.

Half a mile from Hound Tor is Bowerman's Nose, a granite formation said to have been a bowman at the time of the Norman Conquest who – according to which version of the story you hear – fell foul either of the Evil

Huntsman or of a coven of witches and was turned to stone. His hound became Hound Tor, hence the name. There was once a Logan Stone on the top of the Tor – a precariously balanced granite boulder that could be made to rock alarmingly – but vandals managed to unseat it.

Nearby is Jay's Grave, reputed to be the tomb of Mary (or Kitty) Jay, a young orphan girl who became pregnant and hanged herself in shame in the late 18th century. Like all suicides at that time, she was buried at the crossroads to ward off evil spirits. The grave is at the junction of three parishes who all refused to allow her to be buried within their boundaries. When the grave was opened in the 19th century, it did indeed contain the bones of a young girl. The remains were placed in a coffin, reburied at the site and the grave marked with granite stones. The mystery now is that posies of fresh flowers appear on the grave every day, but no-one ever sees them being placed there. Perhaps it is the ghost of James, her childhood friend, who used to collect wild flowers with her – or maybe it's the remorseful spirit of the callous man who seduced and then abandoned her.

A more worrying local phenomenon is the Hairy Hands, said to manifest themselves on the B3212 near Two Bridges and attack travellers. A motorcyclist reported two hairy hands that closed round his own hands on the handlebars and forced him off the road, and a woman in a caravan saw them crawling up her window one evening not so long ago. Locals warn tourists not to stray too close to that road on a moonless night.

ABOVE *Bowerman's Nose, reputed to be a Norman bowman turned to stone by sorcery.*

Berry Pomeroy Castle

DEVON

Berry Pomeroy is the grandaddy of ghost-ridden castles, the most haunted of all. Now a romantic ruin, it has been owned by only two families since the Norman Conquest. At the end of the 11th century it came into the hands of the de Pomeroy family from Normandy, who owned it until 1547 when they sold it to Edward Seymour, first Duke of Somerset, brother of Henry VIII's third queen Jane Seymour, uncle of Edward VI and Lord Protector of England before his disgrace and execution in 1552. His descendants still own the castle today, though it is now in state guardianship.

In the days when it was unlocked and open day and night, it was the regular haunt of ghost-hunters, psychics and dauntless youths out for a thrill. It's got the lot when it comes to cold spots, feelings of fear, pressure on the temples, strange noises and lights and the usual spectral black hound. Real dogs hate being walked near the castle. And it is harmful to modern technology: there are many stories of cameras ceasing to work there, film coming out fuzzy or blank and lighting equipment failing to function. A television camera crew tried for three nights to get shots of the castle, but their cameras jammed. And a photographer reported that a whole reel of film produced excellent shots – except for the one of Berry Pomeroy which was a blank!

On top of all this, the castle has its specific stories. The sounds of galloping hoofbeats followed by cries are reputed to be two Pomeroy brothers who were involved in the religious uprisings of 1549 and were consequently ordered by Edward VI to destroy the castle's defences. When troops arrived to enforce the order, the brothers dressed themselves up in full armour, blindfolded their horses and galloped them over the brink of the precipice to a terrible death.

More sinister is the White Lady, reputedly the ghost of Lady Margaret Pomeroy who was imprisoned by her sister, Lady Eleanor, and starved to death in the room at the base of the tower that still bears her name – Margaret's Tower. The sisters had both fallen in love with the same man, hence Eleanor's jealousy, and Margaret's ghost – dressed all in white and with her hair streaming behind her in disarray – appears both in the room where she was imprisoned and on the Rampart Walk. She is a malevolent presence, appearing only at night and instilling great feelings of fear in those who see her.

Berry Pomeroy specialises in malevolence. Worse even than the White Lady is the Lady in Blue, who predicts the death of those who see her. She is said to be the ghost of a Pomeroy daughter who bore a child to her own father and strangled it. The cries of the child have also been heard. God's wrath at Berry Pomeroy's evil reputation is said to be the reason why the castle is so ruinous today.

Muchelney Abbey

SOMERSET

A romantic legend almost to rival the tale of Romeo and Juliet is set in this Benedictine Abbey, built on one of the 'holy islands' of the Somerset Levels – areas of higher ground in the surrounding marshes where several religious houses, including Glastonbury, were founded. The abbey was originally established in the 7th century by Ine, King of Wessex, and was probably destroyed by the Danes before being refounded around 950 and surviving for nearly six centuries until the Dissolution.

The story is related in a Gothick poem, 'Christabel', by W H Greene. Herbert, the Prior of Muchelney Abbey, walked one day to the nearby nunnery of Westover to perform his regular duty of hearing the nuns' confessions. Sitting in the dark confines of the confessional booth, he was listening to the normal offerings of white lies and petty faults when a nun came in and sobbingly confessed that the love of a man was making her forget her love of God.

Pray for me! Pray! Oh, I am lost through love!
Pray for me! Pray! For I forget my God!

The Prior thrilled to a memory of his own long-lost love, and begged her to tell her tale. She revealed how she had grown up with a young man who was her soulmate through childhood and into adulthood. But the boy's father declared that he had chosen a rich bride for him and the young lovers were forced to part. Soon after, she was told that her lover had died and she was prostrated with grief. She joined the nunnery, but yet could never believe that her lover was really dead – something still seemed to call her and she could still feel his hands reaching out for her.

OPPOSITE *Sinister Berry Pomeroy Castle, one of the most haunted sites in England.* **LEFT** *Bricked-up masonry in the South Cloister Walk at Muchelney Abbey.*

Oh, wretched me, that dared those oaths to take,
That break them hourly, leaving God for earth.
In all my dreams, 'tis Herbert still I see!

It is, of course, her Herbert who is hearing her story. Throwing back his cowl, he cries with emotion: 'Christabel! Behold: Thy heart hath told thee true. Thy Herbert lives!' His family had told him the same lie, that she was dead, and so he too had taken religious vows.

The lovers soon decide to defy their vows and flee. Herbert knew of a narrow, dark cell under Muchelney Abbey that was never used because a ghostly presence was said to walk the corridor outside it and vanish when it got to the door. He brought Christabel to this place under the concealment of a dark winter night, locked her in and went to join his brothers at their evening devotions before returning for her. But her escape had been discovered and he, with all the other monks, was forced to take part in the search for her. Meanwhile she cowered in the cell, enduring the freezing cold and the fear of the ghostly horror that haunted her hiding place, and slowly sank into death. Herbert returned too late to her marble corpse, and

He kissed her tenderly: then rose and went,
Unnoticed in the darkness, and ne'er more
Was seen at Muchelney.

Years later, a 'haggard hermit, stark and dead' was found in a gloomy cell in a wild mountain pass in Wales. He wore on his breast a tress of a woman's hair wrapped in a scrap of parchment on which was written one word: Christabel!

Glastonbury Tor

SOMERSET

Few places are more surrounded in mystery and mysticism than Glastonbury Tor, that high hill dominating the flat lands of Somerset around it, surmounted by the tower of the medieval church – all that is now left of this important medieval abbey and centre of Christian worship and pilgrimage. Jesus himself, accompanying his uncle Joseph of Arimathea, is said to have founded the first church here.

Once regularly surrounded by water and accessible only by a narrow causeway, Glastonbury Tor is suffused with legends. It is said to be the home of Gwyn ap Nudd, King of the Underworld and Lord of the Wild Hunt, and his fairy kingdom. The entrance to the kingdom is reputed to be hidden somewhere on the Tor, but woe betide anyone who finds it and pays the fairies a visit: when they return to the land of humans they are likely to find that years have passed and all those they knew and loved have grown old and died. Anyone rash enough to partake of the fairies' hospitality by eating or drinking while in their kingdom never returns at all.

Avalon is the name of the fairy kingdom, and it was to Avalon that King Arthur was taken after he suffered his last mortal wound at the Battle of Camlann. He and Queen Guinevere were reported to have been buried on Glastonbury Tor; bones dug up by the monks of Glastonbury Abbey in the 13th century were believed to be theirs, and were reburied in a black marble tomb in front of the high altar of the church. The remains disappeared at the Dissolution and were never seen again.

The Holy Grail is reputed to be at Glastonbury too: the cup from which Jesus drank at the Last Supper and was used by Joseph of Arimathea to collect his blood at the Crucifixion was allegedly brought here by Joseph and buried. The quest to find it was one of the preoccupations of King Arthur and his knights, and its burial place is said to be near the Chalice Well at the foot of the Tor where the water runs red with blood (or iron oxide). Joseph also left another memorial: he stuck his staff into the ground before going to sleep, and in the morning found that it had sprouted into the Glastonbury Thorn, still to be found

growing on the Tor. It blooms twice a year, in May and at Christmas.

After Arthur's death, the Tor was haunted by a knight in black armour with glowing red eyes, whose mission was to destroy all records of King Arthur's life and victories – which is why so little is now known about him! Guinevere, too, has been seen here, surrounded by a golden light. Arthur himself is said to haunt Hunting Causeway, a path running along a ley line between Glastonbury and Cadbury Castle, leading his band of knights on Christmas Eve. And there have been numerous sightings of balls of light, of all sizes and colours, hovering over the Tor and along the ley lines, so many of which apparently converge here. Two separate groups of people saw a shining orange ball during the solar eclipse in 1999. Glowing lights also sometimes delineate the spiral pathway that runs up the Tor... a magical place indeed!

ABOVE *Glastonbury Tor. It is here, in the magical kingdom of Avalon that the Holy Grail is believed to be hidden.*

Creech Hill

SOMERSET

This part of Somerset is full of tales of mystery, rooted in strange places like Creech Hill where, in the remains of a Romano-Celtic temple on the summit, two crossed bodies were discovered in the 18th century.

The hill has an evil reputation, and is said to be the haunt of a boggart – or bullbeggar, to give it its local name – which manifests itself as a gruesome black shape that screeches and shrieks with manic laughter. A farmer once came across what he thought was an injured man lying beside the road, but when he approached to offer help it rose up to an immense height above him and emitted a fearsome scream. The farmer fled, but the thing followed him, and he only just reached the safety of his home. As his wife tried to comfort him she caught sight of the long black figure bounding back up the hill, laughing inanely.

Another man had no choice other than to cross the hill one night, despite its reputation. As he marched firmly up the hill, armed with a stout stick, he suddenly felt deathly cold and something tall and black rose up out of the ground in front of him. He struck out at it but his stick went straight through it and he found himself transfixed to the spot. Surrounded by incessant peals of awful laughter, he was unable to free himself until a distant cock crowed at the first light of morning.

ABOVE *A gruesome black shape that shrieks with manic laughter haunts the summit of Creech Hill.*

OPPOSITE *Sherborne Old Castle, where the headless ghost of Sir Walter Raleigh is seen.*

Sherborne Old Castle

DORSET

Built in the 12th century by Roger de Caen, the powerful Bishop of Salisbury, Sherborne Old Castle was also the residence of Sir Walter Raleigh to whom Queen Elizabeth I granted the estate in 1592. The castle was held for the king in the Civil War, and was eventually stormed in 1645 and then dismantled.

Raleigh was executed while in possession of Sherborne Old Castle, and his headless ghost is said to return to the castle at midnight on Michaelmas Eve, 29 September, walking the grounds that were so dear to him when he lived there.

Fiddleford Manor

DORSET

Many different ghostly phenomena have been reported at this fine medieval hall with its open timber roof. The custodian of the manor in the 1980s reported several supernatural encounters including footsteps coming from the solar, although there was no-one there when he investigated. Then, in 1988, there was a flurry of phantom sightings after workmen lifted floorboards while installing a central heating system. One was a man dressed in a brown robe with a leather apron round his waist and a flat black velvet hat on his head. Another sighting was of a knight in armour who carried a white shield with an unusual red crest emblazoned upon it. He had also been seen when Fiddleford Manor was being restored in the 1960s. As soon as the work on the central heating system had finished, and the floorboards were relaid, the spectral visitations ceased.

Athelhampton Hall

DORSET

This fine house, one of the best examples in the country of 15th-century domestic architecture, has been a family home for centuries. The crest of its owners, the Martyn family, was an ape sitting on a tree stump, and it is the ghost of a monkey that is said to haunt it now. As the story goes, a young woman of the family was jilted in love and decided to kill herself. She climbed a stairway behind a secret doorway in the Great Chamber to a room where she could be alone, and there sorrowfully committed suicide. But she had not noticed that the family pet, a monkey, had followed her and was trapped. It starved to death, and can now be heard scratching the panelling of the secret stairway.

There is a grey lady too, who has often been seen in the Tudor Room. One housemaid saw her sitting there in a chair and, thinking that she was a visitor, asked her to leave as it was late in the day. She was amazed when the lady got up and left – through the panelling. Other ghosts include a priest in a hooded black robe, phantom duellists and a cooper who hammers away at ghostly casks in the wine cellars.

ABOVE *A pet monkey haunts Athelhampton Hall, the ancestral home of the Martyn family.*
ABOVE RIGHT *Sculpture, Lulworth Castle.*

Lulworth Castle

DORSET

This early 17th-century hunting lodge, transformed in the 18th century into a splendid country house, was the home of the Weld family for centuries. Tradition has it that they were being stalked down the years by a mysterious grey lady, but no-one knew who she was or why she was so fixated on them. When a disastrous fire struck the castle in 1929, one of the estate workers heard the distressed cries of a woman coming from the window of a burning upstairs room, but when he hastily ran a ladder up to rescue her she was nowhere to be seen and it was clear that the floor of the room had collapsed many hours before. Could this have been the mysterious stalker?

Lulworth has its ration of more out-of-the-way tales too, including a strange glowing room which shone brightly at night for no obvious reason. When it was eventually decided to get rid of the phenomenon by knocking the room down and rebuilding it, the new room started glowing again immediately. And there is – or was – a statue in the park of a Roman soldier who was said to climb down from his plinth every day and go into the castle for his lunch.

Knowlton Church and Earthworks

DORSET

The transition from pre-Christian religious beliefs to Christianity was often a gradual process and is sometimes symbolised by the continued use of sacred places. Some Christian churches were built next to standing stones, and at Knowlton the Norman church was built in the centre of a Neolithic earthwork, once part of a triple henge. Now ruined, the church was last used in 1647.

Some people visiting at twilight or at night have heard singing coming from the church. But the main story connected with Knowlton concerns the church bells, of which there were three. There are many tales about bells being irretrievably sunk into deep pools or rivers, some perhaps deliberately at the time of the Reformation to save them from Henry VIII's despoilers, while others were stolen and yet others, as legend has it, immersed themselves voluntarily in protest at Henry's actions. Names like Bell Hole or Bell Pool are the relics of these legends.

One of the bells of Knowlton Church is said to lie in Bell Hole, otherwise known as White Mill Hole, near Shapwick. It is said that the bell-ringers of Sturminster Marshall stole the bell one snowy night and, nervous of being detected, reversed the shoes of their horses to baffle pursuers. At White Mill Bridge, two of the party went ahead to make sure that the way was clear, and when they failed to return the others decided to cut their losses and throw the bell into White Mill Hole.

The people of Knowlton made three attempts to recover their bell but each time, when it came within reach, the rope broke for no apparent reason. In the end they gave up in despair, and a local saying commemorates this:

All the devils in Hell
Could never pull up Knowlton Bell

On dark and stormy nights, the Knowlton Bell can still be heard ringing in the depths of White Mill Hole.

OPPOSITE *Knowlton Church*
where a ghostly bell still tolls.

Old Wardour Castle

WILTSHIRE

One of the many casualties of the Civil War was Old Wardour Castle which was besieged twice, in 1643 and 1644. There is no other castle in England like Old Wardour, with its hexagonal plan; like Nunney Castle nearby, it was clearly designed on French lines. The story of the sieges is also unusual, in that the defender on the first occasion was Lady Blanche Arundell, who was about 60 at the time. Her husband was away in Oxford when the Parliamentarians besieged the castle, and she refused to surrender despite the fact that she had a garrison of only 25 men against a force of 1,300, and although there were many women and children living in the castle. They held out against batterings from cannon and mining for several days before finally giving in. Lady Blanche's husband died shortly afterwards, from a wound sustained while fighting for the king at the Battle of Lansdowne, and his widow, left destitute after the siege, was provided with lodgings in Salisbury. She died in 1649.

The Parliamentarian victors did a great deal of damage to the castle, and a lot more was done during the second siege, this time by the Royalists, led by Lady Blanche's son, against the Parliamentarian garrison. Although the Arundell family regained the estate at the Restoration in 1660, they never repaired the castle, preferring to build a smaller house nearby. They were staunch adherents of the old Roman Catholic religion – a Catholic chaplain was present during the first siege, and drew up the terms of capitulation – and it is likely that Wardour is one of the few places in England where the 'old religion' never ceased to be practised. The last Lord Arundell died in 1944.

White owls at Old Wardour are said to have been harbingers of death to the heads of the family, and the indomitable Lady Blanche herself is sometimes seen, walking at twilight across the terrace of the old castle to the lake.

ABOVE *Sculpture, Old Wardour Castle.*

OPPOSITE *Old Wardour Castle, where white owls were said to have been harbingers of death to the Arundell family.*

Nunney Castle

SOMERSET

This castle, with its carp-filled moat, is the stuff of fairy tales, its towers and massive walls looming over the small village houses surrounding it. Like Old Wardour, the building shows a strong French influence and in its heyday would have looked much more like the castle that housed Sleeping Beauty in the Disney cartoon – or, in real life, the reconstructed Old City of Carcassonne in the south of France – than its solid English counterparts.

It did, however, see violent action during the Civil War, albeit for only two days. In 1645 its owner, the Royalist Colonel Prater, defied a Parliamentarian force which arrived to besiege it as part of a general clearing-up operation in the area. The situation was complicated by the fact that the Royalist defenders were Catholics, while many of the villagers were Parliamentarian Protestants – one of whom may have used his inside knowledge of the castle's construction to inform the attackers that the north wall was a weak point. Cannon fire was directed against that wall and within hours the wall was breached and the defenders surrendered.

There is a sub-plot. It seems that one of those inside the castle was a Royalist woman who had conducted an affair with the Parliamentarian Puritan village minister. She seems to have been a wandering vagabond, and was inevitably accused by the villagers of being a witch. When the castle fell, she was tied up and thrown into a nearby stream, the traditional trial for a witch. When she floated, her guilt was proved and she was burned to death on a great pyre in the shadow of the castle walls. Her ghostly figure remains for ever doomed to wander the villages of Nunney and nearby Mells – which has the distinction of being the most haunted village in Somerset.

OPPOSITE *The remains of the fairy-tale castle at Nunney.*

Stanton Drew Stone Circles

SOMERSET

Stanton Drew, dating from the Neolithic period (about 5,000 years ago), consists of three circles, two avenues, the set of three stones known as the Cove and an outlier known as Hautville's Quoit. The Great Circle is the second largest stone circle in Britain after Avebury. One of the other two circles is in a very ruinous condition, but the complex remains much as it was when recorded over 300 years ago by the antiquarian William Stukeley (1687–1765). It is, however, a much more elaborate and impressive monument than was known until recently: a scientific survey in 1998 showed that there are no fewer than nine concentric circles of pits under the grass within the Great Circle, many of which would have held massive posts, and that the Great Circle itself is contained within a huge buried enclosure ditch. The whole would have formed an enormous and important ritual landscape.

Despite the fact that the Great Circle clearly comprises 27 stones – many of them now recumbent – as usual it is supposed to be impossible to count them. Any attempt leads to death or sickness, and in 1750 one John Wood reported that when he started to count the stones a great thunderstorm started. And as usual, the stones are said to be the petrified remains of people, here a bridal party who wanted to carry on their revels after midnight into the Sabbath. When the fiddler refused to carry on playing, the drunken bride swore that she would even go to hell to find a replacement. When an old man turned up agreeing to play, the guests were compelled by his frenzied playing to dance on and on until dawn – when, of course, the old man was revealed as the Devil, the revelers were turned to stone and he made off with their souls. The three stones forming the Cove, which sit behind the church in the garden of the pub, are said to be the bride, the groom and the drunken parson lying in a stupor at their feet. As he left, the Devil promised to return and play again, but until he does the party-goers are condemned to their cold vigil.

Farleigh Hungerford Castle

SOMERSET

The castle still bears the name of the Hungerford family who built it in the late 14th century. The family had mixed fortunes: one of them, Robert, was captured and imprisoned in France at the end of the Hundred Years War, and when he returned to England he joined the Lancastrian cause in the Wars of the Roses and was attainted and executed. The attainder (seizure of property) was reversed when his grandson was on the winning side at the Battle of Bosworth in 1485, and had the castle returned to him by the new King Henry VII. But the family lost the castle irrevocably in the middle of the 16th century when Walter Hungerford was accused by his wife of trying to poison her and imprisoning her in the tower still known as The Lady's Tower. He was eventually accused of treason and 'unnatural vice', and executed.

The castle is said to be haunted by the ghost of Lady Agnes Hungerford who, in order to be free to marry Sir Edward Hungerford, is said to have had her first husband strangled and his body burnt in the castle kitchen. But the crime was discovered after Sir Edward's death in 1522, and she and an accomplice were found guilty of the murder and hanged at Tyburn. She is said to wander mournfully around the castle near the chapel.

One of Farleigh Hungerford's mysteries concerns the small group of burials in lead coffins still to be seen behind the grille of the small crypt. Encased in body-shaped lead, some of them are presumably women who died in childbirth, since the tiny coffins of babies are perched on top of them. They are wearing lead masks which may have been moulded from their actual faces. It is believed that they are the inner coffins of members of the Hungerford family who died in the mid-17th century. But their names are forgotten, and it is not known how they have managed to survive the ravages of the centuries.

West Kennet Long Barrow

WILTSHIRE

This Neolithic chambered tomb, situated high above Avebury and Silbury Hill, was in use for over 1,000 years before being sealed in about 2200 BC. The tomb itself consists of five chambers, two on each side of a central passage which opens out into a fifth chamber at the end. These chambers stretch a mere 10 metres or so into the mound which is over 100 metres long.

The remains of over 40 individuals were found in the chambers when they were excavated. Many of them had been moved aside to make room for later interments, and it is notable that many bones – mostly skulls and legs – had been removed and taken elsewhere. Some of the bones were arranged in what appeared to be a formal manner, but others had apparently just been kicked aside. It is possible that the dead people buried here – who are likely to have been the elite of the community – had been exposed to rot in the open air in the ritual known as excarnation before their bones were placed in the tomb.

West Kennet is said to be haunted by a white spectral figure accompanied by a white dog with red ears who have been seen entering the tomb at sunrise on Midsummer's Day. Is it possible that this is a lingering folk memory of the days when the barrow was the scene of midsummer rituals?

Haunted Salisbury

WILTSHIRE

Debenham's in Salisbury is the only department store in the world that can boast both an execution site under its foundations and the active 500-year-old ghost of one of those beheaded there. The unfortunate man was the Duke of Buckingham, executed in Salisbury's marketplace in 1483 on the orders of Richard III. His still bleeding head was taken to be shown to the king who was staying in the Cathedral Close, where the bloodstains sometimes still manifest themselves even today. And the headless spirit still haunts the site of his grisly death; only recently a British Telecom engineer was working alone in one of the unused attic rooms at the store when he distinctly felt a cold hand touch his shoulder. He fled in terror and could not be persuaded back into the room at any cost; one of his colleagues had to go back in there to fetch his tools.

National Monuments Record Centre

SWINDON, WILTSHIRE

English Heritage's offices in Swindon were once railway buildings, part of Brunel's magnificent Great Western Railway. While they were still being used for their original purpose they were regularly patrolled by security guards with dogs. One night in the early 1990s the guard heard the sound of a clock being wound and went to investigate. He saw a man with his back to him clearly operating a winding key, though there was no clock on the wall. He challenged him – and the figure turned round to reveal that he had no face.

Understandably, the guard fled and had to be admitted to hospital with shock. His dog fared even worse; it was so traumatised by the incident that it eventually had to be put down. It seems that there had indeed been a clock on that wall during the building's earlier heyday as railway offices, and that it had needed regularly winding with a key. And to this day, even the large, fierce dogs used by security firms will not go near the place where the apparition was seen. Nor, oddly, will most dogs allow themselves to be led through the door that is now the main entrance to the building; almost all of them pull away and will not go through that door or the passage beyond it.

Avebury Stone Circles

WILTSHIRE

All stone circles have their numinous qualities, and Avebury has the additional mysteriousness of enclosing the village which has grown up within it. Its huge circles of stones and still-deep ditches – the largest stone circle in the world – sit firmly within the landscape of houses and roads, an inescapable part of the community.

Many of the stones have been re-erected within the last hundred years, after they were buried in medieval times to hide their pagan associations from good Christian eyes. One unfortunate man who may have been involved in this medieval work was a travelling barber-surgeon whose skeleton was found under one of the stones when it was lifted in 1938. He still had his medical probe, some scissors and a few 13th-century coins, and he had clearly been crushed when the stone was toppled. The bones were

for many years thought to have been lost, the victim of a wartime air raid on the Royal College of Surgeons where they were being studied. But they had been removed for safe-keeping to the Natural History Museum where they were found among a collection of skeletons in 1999.

Some local people have seen small figures flitting around the stones at the time of the full moon, and strange lights and music have also been heard. What appeared to be the ghost of a whole fair was also seen in 1916 by a woman who wanted to visit the stones but was put off by the bustle and noise; it was only later that she realised that the last fair held at Avebury had been in the 1850s. In truth, Avebury needs no ghosts: the tingle factor lies inescapably in the age and antiquity of the stones themselves, set within and around the modern community.

Stonehenge

WILTSHIRE

Perhaps the world's most famous prehistoric monument, and now, with Avebury, a World Heritage Site, Stonehenge has for centuries teased and fascinated those who have sought to discover who built it and what it was for. We do now know quite a lot about it: archaeology has revealed much about its age and how it was constructed. The recent discovery nearby of a burial containing the remains of a number of people whose origin can be traced to the Preseli area of Wales supports the geological analysis of the bluestones of the inner circle, which revealed that the stones did indeed come from the Preseli mountains. The sarsens that form the massive trilithons are readily available in the neighbouring countryside, and experiments have demonstrated how the stones were dragged to the site and erected. Dating techniques allow us to be pretty clear about the various phases of the monument – and to recognise and marvel at the engineering skills of the people who built it.

But we can never know exactly why it was built – and therein lies its fascination! Early antiquarians thought it was a Druid temple, a theory disproved when dating evidence revealed that it was far older than the period when these Iron Age priests flourished. This does not of course prevent modern Druids claiming it as their own, nor the belief that it was the scene of ghoulish Druidic rituals involving human sacrifice. William Stukeley was the first to speculate that it was a giant astronomical calendar, and the rising of the midsummer sun over the Heel Stone every year attracts thousands of worshippers of all kinds. Ley lines are said to converge here, and the land around is a magnet for the creators of crop circles, be they alien or terrestrial. The discovery of a carving of a dagger on one of the stones prompted the suggestion – because of its superficial resemblance to the daggers of that civilisation – that the people of Bronze Age Mycenae in Greece had been its builders. Other candidates include the inhabitants of the drowned city of Atlantis.

Dancing giants is another possibility: a ring of giants dancing in a circle with arms linked at shoulder level were suddenly, and inexplicably, turned to stone. And of course there's the Devil. The story goes that an old woman in Ireland had all these huge stones in her garden, and the Devil coveted them. So he approached her with a bag of gold coins and offered to buy the stones for as much of the gold as she could count while he transported them. She agreed, whereupon he used his devilish powers to spirit them away in an instant – and she got nothing.

Proud of his new monument, he challenged the local people to guess how many stones there were. A local friar guessed right, whereupon the angry Devil hurled one of the monoliths at him, only to see it deflected off the friar's heel: hence the Heel Stone, with its foot-shaped dent.

The involvement of Merlin, Arthur and the British kings is another tale, told by Geoffrey of Monmouth in the 12th century. According to this story, Hengist, the Saxon who had invaded and subjugated part of Britain, devised a wicked plan to consolidate his hold on the kingdom. He summoned the princes of the British tribes to a convocation on Salisbury Plain, and murdered them there. This led to the Battle of Mons Badonicus where the Saxons were defeated by the British, led by King Arthur. Visiting the burial place of the slain princes after the battle, Arthur was moved to tears and asked Merlin what memorial he should erect for them. Merlin suggested the Dance of the Giants on Mount Killaraus in Ireland, and Arthur sent an army to appropriate this huge stone circle. The Irish king objected, but he was defeated and the stones were moved by Merlin's magic powers to Salisbury Plain where they stand sentinel over the British princes. It is said that Uther Pendragon, Constantine and Ambrosius – powerful British rulers of the 6th century – are buried there too.

Bodies have indeed been discovered both at Stonehenge and nearby, including recently a warrior whose DNA proved that he had originally come from Europe. And work on a skeleton excavated at Stonehenge in 1923 showed that he was a local man who had been beheaded with a sharp sword sometime in the 7th or 8th century AD. Human sacrifice, or maybe just a common criminal – who knows?

'Tis a fearful thing to be no more,
    Or if it be, to wander after death;
To walk, as spirits do, in brakes all day;
    And when the darkness comes to glide in paths
That lead to graves; and, in the silent vault,
    Where lies your own pale shroud, to hover o'er it,
Striving to enter your forbidden corpse.

JOHN DRYDEN

Medieval Merchant's House, Southampton

HAMPSHIRE

An incredible legacy from the 12th century that has survived time and Southampton's devastation by bombing during the Second World War, this timber-framed house was once the shop and home of a prosperous merchant. Situated in French Street, the High Street of the time, this house is the focus of ley lines and mysterious sightings. Visitors have seen a tall man in a black hat near the fireplace in the hall and a small girl in the corner of the front bedroom.

There is a mystery in the cellar too: in the mid-1990s footprints started to appear without reason in a gravelled area next to a blocked-up doorway. Even after the loose gravel was raked smooth and the door to the cellar locked, new footprints appeared in the gravel. A few days later further footprints appeared. The prints varied in length and depth and none seemed to have been made in a walking sequence. Some of the shapes seemed to have been made with a pointed shoe, while others were squarer as though made with a patten rather than a shoe. No explanation has ever been found.

Netley Abbey

HAMPSHIRE

Founded in the 13th century, Netley Abbey had by the early 18th century become a romantic ruin and was sold to a builder who intended to demolish it for its stone. Just as work was beginning, the builder had a dream that the keystone from one of the arches fell on him, but he carried on regardless. All work on the demolition of the abbey had to cease, however, when he was indeed killed by a stone falling from one of the window arches. Not surprisingly, a superstition soon grew up that a curse would fall on those who dared to take the abbey's stones – which is perhaps why so much of it remains today.

The abbey is renowned for its cold spots and sudden drops in temperature, and is said to be the haunt of 'blind Peter' who is sometimes seen near the sacristy.

PREVIOUS PAGE LEFT *Detail from an urn, Battle Abbey.*
PREVIOUS PAGE RIGHT *Cowdray Park, Sussex.*
OPPOSITE *The spectral shell of Netley Abbey.*

Carisbrooke Castle

ISLE OF WIGHT

Situated right in the centre of the Isle of Wight, this immensely strong 12th-century fortress has dominated the island for centuries, and was hugely significant in the defence of the realm against the threats from the French and Spanish in the late Middle Ages. One of its roles was as the prison where Charles I was held before being taken to London for his trial and execution. He made two attempts to escape, and was only foiled on the first occasion when he got stuck in the bars of the window of his room, which he had attempted to squeeze through in the mistaken belief that where his head could pass his body would follow. On his second attempt he burnt through the bars with acid and was about to climb out when his jailer, Colonel Hammond, arrived with the words: 'I am come to take leave of your majesty, for I hear you are going away.' The room where Charles was held can still be seen at the castle, though the window has long gone; he was held there until 6 September 1648, when he started the journey to London for his trial in the Palace of Westminster and his beheading on a scaffold outside the Banqueting Hall at Whitehall Palace on 30 January 1649.

The tread-wheel, which operates the machinery of the well-house, was initially worked by prisoners but since the late 17th century donkeys have been used instead. Donkeys are still there today, still working the wheel, though now for the benefit of tourists rather than thirsty castle inhabitants. The well-house is haunted by the ghost

OPPOSITE *Carisbrooke Castle. This haunted fortress is where Charles I was held prisoner before his eventual execution in 1649.*

OPPOSITE *The much-haunted Osborne House on the Isle of Wight, the home of Queen Victoria and Prince Albert.*
RIGHT *Bronze statue in the gardens of Osborne House.*
OVERLEAF *A decorative urn, flanked by winged sphinxes, in the gardens of Osborne House.*

of a young woman whose disembodied face, surrounded by what appear to be the billowing draperies of her dress, has been glimpsed in the waters of the deep well. A woman who saw the apparition was overwhelmed by huge feelings of pity and grief; it was only later that she found out that a young woman called Elizabeth Ruffin had indeed drowned in the well in the early 17th century. She felt that the ghost was calling out to her, telling that she had not killed herself but that her death was a tragic accident.

The castle has other ghosts as well. A young man in a brown jerkin, who has often been seen near the moat, actually spoke in a strange dialect to one of those who saw him. A woman in Victorian dress was clearly seen by a couple who were strolling round the castle, appearing to glide above the ground and with two shadowy dogs on leashes. And there is another figure often seen in the courtyard, wearing a long coat and with four tiny lap dogs. She was seen one hot day by two members of a school party, who separately remarked on the heaviness of her clothing, given the weather.

Osborne House
ISLE OF WIGHT

Osborne House, the beloved country home of Queen Victoria and Prince Albert, was built on the site of an earlier Georgian manor house, and it is possible that some of the ghosts that now inhabit it date to that earlier building. The royal nurseries on the top floor are the scene of several manifestations. One custodian saw a man dressed in Georgian clothes walking out of the wall of one of the rooms, and another sighting was of a man in a silvery-grey suit and narrow trousers – more Victorian in style – emerging through a locked door. The custodian clearly saw his right arm and leg, before he retreated quickly when she challenged him. The room in question, which was always kept locked, was the one used by Victoria's delicate haemophiliac son, Prince Leopold. A shadow frequently seen passing along the corridors outside the nurseries is also believed to be the spirit of Leopold.

Towards the end of Queen Victoria's life her daughter Princess Beatrice lived with her at Osborne,

together with her husband, Prince Henry of Battenburg. The princess has been seen standing in the window of the room that had been her bedroom, dressed in a black Edwardian-style gown, and a lady in a white ball-dress has been seen in the corridor outside the room, moving along silently with her gown swaying around her. The queen had several Indian servants after being crowned Empress of India, and one of them, a little Indian boy, has been seen near the Durbar Room, wearing a turban, a long greenish-blue jacket and silky trousers. And Queen Victoria herself sometimes manifests herself in her bedroom through the strong scent of her favourite jasmine and orange-blossom; the scent is so strong that visitors remark on it.

Two tragedies befalling servants of the house appear to have left their mark. A custodian who was alone in the house one Saturday morning heard a scream and a loud thump coming from a nearby steep stone staircase which was kept roped off because it was regarded as dangerous. When he rushed outside to investigate there was no-one there, and it was only later that he learned that a parlour maid had been killed in a fall on that staircase in the 1880s. Another fatality took place in the Table Deckers' Room in the basement, where a servant girl reportedly hanged herself; staff stationed in the room, which is now open to the public, report chill feelings and a sensation of being watched.

Rooms imbued with heavy feelings of oppressive dread... shadows flitting just out of the corner of the eye in the Horn Room, where Queen Victoria used to sit with her servant John Brown and an ouija board, trying to conjure up the spirit of her beloved dead Albert... the feeling of being touched when there is no-one there... the sound of children's laughter near the Swiss Cottage where the royal children played... footsteps pattering across empty basement rooms.... Those working at Osborne are well used to all of this. 'Oh it's just the ghosts,' they say. 'We hear them all the time. We're used to them now.'

Highly haunted island

The Isle of Wight is reputed to be one of the most haunted places in England, with a wealth of spectres of all ages. At East Cowes, near Osborne, a headless Second World War airman has been seen on several occasions, parachuting in from the skies. And the grand Royal Yacht Squadron in what was Cowes Castle has two ghosts: one a soldier in an old-fashioned uniform with a pillbox hat under his arm, and the other the Marquis of Anglesey, who lived there until his death in 1854.

A floating decapitated head was seen in the 1920s at Billingham Manor, coinciding with the execution of a prisoner at Parkhurst Jail – and another prisoner there, who committed suicide, returned afterwards to his old cell and sat on his bunk with his legs hanging over the edge. His fellow lags were so spooked that they clamoured to be moved from that cell. Some ghosts have names: the acclaimed pioneer of photography, Julia Margaret Cameron, is still seen at her old home, Dimbola Lodge, wearing a brown taffeta dress that can be heard rustling as she moves. More sinister is Michael Morey, who brutally murdered his grandson and was tried and executed for the crime at Winchester. His corpse was brought back to Gallows Hill, Downend, where it was left to rot on the gibbet there. The gibbet crossbeam is still to be seen at the nearby Hare and Hounds pub, with a notch in it and the date of his execution inscribed, and Morey himself is said to prowl Gallows Hill, carrying a huge axe. And there's the dripping ghost of the drowned seaman who stumbles out of the sea at the Back of the Wight beaches, and the ruined manor of Knighton Gorges which reappears on New Year's Eve accompanied by poltergeists, flashing lights and the sounds of revelry...

OPPOSITE *The massive fortified walls of Porchester Castle.*

Portchester Castle

HAMPSHIRE

Like many of the fortifications built along the south coast, Portchester has a long history. Originally built by the Romans as part of their Saxon Shore string of defences against the Saxon marauders from the sea, it was continually adapted and refortified right up until the Napoleonic Wars when it was used to house French prisoners. It was the base from which Edward I set out for his French campaigns, and also saw Henry V's departure for Agincourt in 1415. More recently, its large grassy compound provided an ideal ground for early cricket matches between the garrison and sailors from the navy anchored outside its walls – matches re-enacted recently with full competitive fervour by modern teams in uncomfortable Georgian dress.

Portchester's varied history has resulted in several varieties of ghost. There is the ubiquitous monk, and a phantom woman bending over a grave in the church in the grounds, as well as more nebulous sightings of vague whitish shapes at dusk.

Portsmouth

HAMPSHIRE

The guest smartly dressed in a brown tweed suit, with a pork-pie hat on his head and a silver-mounted sword-stick in his hand is a regular at the Sally Port Hotel in Portsmouth. In fact, he's reputedly been visiting since 1956 – the year he died! The sword-stick is a clue to the identity of this ghost because engraved upon it is a crab. 'Crabbie' was the nickname of Lieutenant Commander Lionel Kenneth Philip Crabb, one of the Royal Navy's top frogmen who had distinguished himself during the Second World War defusing underwater mines. He had been awarded the George Cross for his bravery and later earned the OBE. And after his demob in 1947 he seems to have become involved in espionage for the British government.

Crabb was staying at the Sally Port Hotel in 1956 when the Soviet Premier Nikita Khrushchev and Marshal Bulganin arrived in Portsmouth on a goodwill visit to Britain aboard the Russian cruiser *Ordzhonikidze*. At this time the Cold War was at its height and relations between the two countries were tense and laced with suspicion. Crabb appears to have been told to secretly inspect the hull of the Russian ship while it was in Portsmouth harbour, and this he apparently did – but he was never seen again. The alarm was raised when he failed to appear for breakfast the next day, but then it was discovered that his hotel room had been mysteriously cleared and the bill paid. His disappearance led to a major diplomatic incident and intense press speculation and interest. What had been Crabb's fate? Had he been discovered spying and killed by the Russians? Had he been taken prisoner? Had he drowned? There were lots of questions but no answers until many months later when a headless and handless body surfaced from the sea. It was claimed that this was Crabb's corpse, but there was no positive proof and the mystery remains. The ghost at the hotel offers no clues, and the Cabinet Papers concerning the affair won't be available until 2057.

Waverley Abbey

SURREY

This was the first Cistercian monastery in England, founded in 1128. As usual, its resident ghost is a monk, but his story is rather more specific than usual. Said to have been hanged, drawn and quartered, he is sadly searching for his lost entrails. His crime must have been a heinous one to have deserved such a punishment: those who had taken religious vows enjoyed 'benefit of clergy' and often escaped the worst excesses of the law.

OPPOSITE *The skeletal ruins of Waverley Abbey.*

OPPOSITE *Bramber Castle, where*
the sad ghosts of two starving
children have been seen.

Bramber Castle

WEST SUSSEX

This early Norman motte-and-bailey castle was built in
the 11th century by William de Braoise, and little now
remains. It stayed in the same family until 1324, and there
is a story that a later de Braoise fell out with King John
who imprisoned him and his wife and children at Windsor
Castle where they all starved to death. In another version
of this tale, de Braoise abandoned his family to their fate
and fled to Ireland.

The ghosts of the children, desperately searching
for food, are said to haunt Bramber Castle in the depths
of winter. They are seen holding their hands out in
supplication, but disappear when approached.

Bramber Castle seems to attract stories of despair.
A later owner, Lord Hubert de Hurst, reputedly
discovered his wife, Maude of Ditchling, with her lover
and had him bricked up alive in the cellar. Maude's howls
of anguish have been heard among the ruins. And more
recently, a woman visiting the castle with her husband
experienced such feelings of terror that nothing would
ever induce her to set foot there again – even though her
husband felt nothing! She was convinced that something
dreadful had happened there, so awful that it left a still
perceptible tremor in the air.

Pevensey Castle

EAST SUSSEX

Like Dover Castle, Pevensey Castle has seen nearly 2,000
years of history from its important strategic position on
the south coast of England, facing the perennial threat
from the Continent. It was where William the Conqueror
landed in 1066 before marching along the coast to the
place now called Battle where he defeated the Saxon King
Harold at the Battle of Hastings. But its history goes back
even further, to the late 3rd century AD when a Roman

fort called Anderida was built here. It is one of the largest Roman forts to survive in Britain, with the massive Roman walls and towers still standing to virtually their full height around most of the perimeter. And it also saw action during the Second World War when, after the fall of France in 1940, an invasion of Britain was a real possibility and the fortifications at Pevensey were strengthened and garrisoned.

So Pevensey's military importance has never receded – a fact that is perhaps reflected in the sounds of spectral battles that have often been heard there, accompanied by brief sightings of large armies. A particular story concerns Lady Joan Pelham, who was the wife of Sir John Pelham, appointed in 1394 as the Constable of Pevensey. He supported Henry Bolingbroke's usurpation of the throne of Richard II in 1399 and went to fight for him, leaving his wife at the castle. When it was besieged by forces loyal to Richard II, she wrote a celebrated letter to her husband asking for help:

My dear lord it is right that you know of my position, I am here laid in manner of a siege… so that I may not out, nor no vitals get without much difficulty. Wherefore my dear may it please you, by the advice of your wise counsel, to give remedy to the salvation of your castle and the malice of your enemies. The Holy Trinity keep you from your enemies and soon send me good tidings of you. Written at Pevensey in the Castle by your own poor J Pelham.

The ghost of the gallant Joan is often to be seen at Pevensey, gliding along the ramparts at dusk.

OPPOSITE *The crumbling Roman walls of Pevensey Castle as twilight descends.*

Battle Abbey

The most memorable date in English history is 1066 – the date of the Battle of Hastings and the last successful invasion of England, by Duke William of Normandy who became William I, 'the Conqueror'. His victory in that momentous battle saw the end of Anglo-Saxon England and the beginnings of deep-rooted French influence on every aspect of life. The date is still viewed as a fundamental turning point in English history, a new start. And the place where it happened resounds with history too.

One of the curious aspects of this major event is that the battle did not actually take place at Hastings, but on Senlac Hill, a strategic ridge on the Sussex Downs a few miles to the north. The place is now called Battle, and is the site of the Benedictine abbey William founded on the site of the conflict to atone for all the blood spilt.

Not surprisingly, paranormal phenomena have frequently been reported over the 1,000 years since this famous battle. The ghost of the Norman knight, Talifer, has been seen, riding in front of the Norman lines, taunting the enemy while singing the 'Song of Roland' before riding a bit too close to the English army and being cut down – 'a brave and romantic knight' or 'a fearless fool', depending on your point of view. And on every 14 October, the anniversary of the battle, the ghost of King Harold – complete with arrow in eye – is said to appear at the place where he fell, the spot later occupied by the high altar of the abbey church. Then, whenever it rains, the battlefield seems to be awash with blood. The rational explanation is that this is merely the iron oxide in the soil mixing with the rainwater, but on a wild, wet October day it is easier to believe that the blood of our Saxon and Norman ancestors is still leaching from the ground where it was spilt.

Battle Abbey became a wealthy religious house, and the town grew up around it to serve the needs of the community. But in 1538 monastic life came to an end when the abbey was forced to surrender to the crown during the Dissolution. The monks had to leave, but it seems that Henry VIII had no control over their spirits since their ghosts have often been seen going about their

OPPOSITE *Battle Abbey, whose ancestral owners, the Browne family, fell victim to an ancient curse.*

everyday business. The abbey has been a school for many years, and photographs taken by visitors have sometimes yielded surprising results. One father snapping his daughter in the common room found a figure in Tudor costume on his film, and a visitor from Zimbabwe, photographing the cloister area, found one photograph marred by a beam of light. On closer examination, the light surrounded a staring face.

After the Dissolution, the abbey and much of its land

were granted to Sir Anthony Browne who was Henry VIII's Master of Horse. He demolished the church, chapter house and part of the cloister and adapted the west range as his residence. Delighted with his new home, Sir Anthony threw a lavish banquet to celebrate, but the revelry came to an abrupt halt when one of the evicted monks burst in. He uttered a curse on the new owners of the abbey saying: 'Mark ye my masters, you shall all die by fire and water.' Over the years various members of the

Browne family met their death by drowning, and in 1931 Battle Abbey was extensively damaged by fire. The 'Curse of Battle Abbey'… or just bad luck? And it was a patient spirit who waited nearly 400 years for his revenge!

It took nearly 900 years, however, for Battle Abbey to have the last word on the Anglo-Norman conflict. It was here that British and Canadian troops were billeted in 1944 during the preparations for the successful Allied invasion of Normandy.

Bayham Old Abbey

KENT

The picturesque ruins of this abbey, built by the Premonstratensian order in the 13th century, are set in a tranquil valley. The ghosts are those usually to be seen at abbey ruins – phantom monks – but here they are sometimes seen en masse, gliding in procession through the abbey, with occasional accompaniments of chanting and bells, and the scent of burning incense. They don't, however, affect the overwhelming peace and serenity of the place – one of the most attractive ruined abbeys in the county, and now much sought after as a memorable venue for weddings.

Dover Castle

KENT

On a clear summer's day, anyone standing on the roof of Dover Castle keep can see the white cliffs of the French coast so clearly that they look as if they are on the other side of a lake. This closeness to France is why Dover has always been so strategically important as the 'gateway to England', the defender of the country against invaders from the Romans on. There is a Roman lighthouse – the Pharos – on the headland next to the Anglo-Saxon church of St Mary-in-Castro, and the castle itself is one of the most impressive in Europe. Built on the site of Iron Age earthworks, the castle dates mostly to the 12th and 13th centuries, but was extensively remodelled in the 18th century and has been in almost constant use throughout its history. The tunnels beneath the castle are as impressive as the buildings on the surface. Some date to

the 13th century and others to the Napoleonic period, and they were in active use during the Second World War when they were the headquarters of Rear-Admiral Ramsay while he was masterminding the evacuation of the British army from Dunkirk. One of the levels has only recently been decommissioned as a Cold War bunker.

It is no surprise that a place where so much has happened has ghosts and legends in abundance. Dover's most famous ghost is the headless drummer boy, seen many times walking the battlements on nights when there is a full moon. No-one knows who he was, but most of the stories place him in the Napoleonic era. One tale has him set upon by thieves while carrying money for the garrison; when he refused to part with the money they cut off his head. He is also reputed to have been a member of a regiment quartered at Dover but to have been killed at the Battle of Waterloo from where his spirit returned to his

former happy home. There are other ghosts too. A lady in red has often been seen peering out of a window in the keep, sometimes so vividly that staff have summoned security guards to check the room which, of course, is empty. Many visitors have seen a Royalist soldier in 17th-century uniform, also in the keep, and there have been sightings of a Roman soldier near the Pharos and a hooded monk hovering near the church.

ABOVE *The repeater station, part of the secret underground tunnels beneath Dover Castle which are now a focus of paranormal phenomena.*

OPPOSITE *The peaceful remains of Bayham Old Abbey witness a procession of ghostly monks and the scent of burning incense.*

The tunnels have their ghosts as well – very recent ones. There have been several sightings of people dressed in Second World War uniforms going about their business in the tunnels, unfazed by modern visitors. Those who have seen them have taken them for re-enactors, and have been shocked and surprised when custodians have told them that no Second World War re-enactors are employed at Dover. Staff members have also seen or felt manifestations in the tunnels, and many of them are unhappy about going into certain parts of the tunnel complex, or locking up on their own. One tour guide was showing people the repeater station, formerly the central radio headquarters, when he heard footsteps behind him and distinctly felt something pass right through his body. One of his group also heard the footsteps and told the guide that he had gone as white as a sheet. There have been so many of these occurrences that paranormal research units have carried out research exercises.

Dover is also one of the many places in England with Arthurian connections, particularly – as related in Malory's 'Morte d'Arthur' – with the conflict towards the end of Arthur's life between the king and his treacherous son (or nephew) Mordred. During Arthur's absence abroad in a French war, Mordred had seized the crown and garrisoned Dover with a great army to prevent his father landing. There was fierce fighting before Mordred was driven back, and it was only at the end of the battle that the great knight Sir Gawaine was discovered severely wounded. Before he died Gawaine wrote a letter to Sir Launcelot, who was overseas, calling him to come to Arthur's aid, and then he was taken to a chapel in Dover Castle where he died and was buried and where his skull could later be seen. Sir Launcelot responded to Gawaine's letter by assembling a huge army and landing at Dover, only to find that he was too late to help King Arthur who had been slain at the Battle of Camlann. Mourning both for the king and Gawaine, Launcelot prayed at the tomb and then announced a great dole of food, wine and money which he dispensed with his own hands, urging everyone who came to pray for Sir Gawaine's soul.

Richborough Roman Fort

KENT

Richborough was the first fort built by the Romans when they invaded Britain in AD 43 during the reign of the Emperor Claudius. The sea has receded since they were here, but Richborough and Reculver were important elements of the Roman coastal defences, and later formed part of the Saxon Shore defence system towards the end of the Roman occupation of Britain when the threat came from the seafaring Saxons.

The still impressive remains – massive walls and deep ditches – are, as is to be expected, the haunt of Roman legionaries: a cohort of Roman soldiers has sometimes been spotted marching between the walls, the sound of their nailed sandals clattering on the paths. But it is perhaps the 'spirit of place' that is the most haunting thing about Richborough. Now rather isolated both from the sea and the settlements around it, and rather overwhelmed by the huge cooling towers of Richborough Power Station, it is an unexpected site as the scene of the very beginning of the Roman occupation of Britain which, although it lasted only about 400 years, had such an enormous effect on the lives of those who lived then and their descendants right down to the present day.

Reculver Towers and Roman Fort

KENT

This adapted Roman fort just along the coast from Richborough was part of the same defensive chain. Its bleak twin towers are all that is now left of the fort after the rest has crumbled into the sea. Many hauntings have been reported here, notably the cries of a baby, reputed to have been buried alive as a sacrifice by the Romans when they built it. Excavations some years ago discovered the skeletons of 11 babies within the ruins.

Ghostly monks have been seen walking across the bridge connecting the towers, and there is also a white figure which floats above the ground and passes through the walls. Those who see it invariably flee in terror as it turns slowly towards them and removes its hood – to reveal that it has no face.

Rochester Castle

KENT

After William the Conqueror had consolidated his hold over England, he rewarded his lords with great tracts of land on which they quickly built castles to control their territories and the unruly populace. Most of these early castles were built of earth and wood in the ubiquitous motte-and-bailey style, but it was not too long before these wooden edifices were replaced by much stronger and more permanent stone structures. The castle at Rochester – in its vitally important position between London and Dover – was one of the first to receive this treatment during the reign of the Conqueror's hated son William II. It may have needed this extra strength because it was the stronghold of Odo, Bishop of Bayeux, who tried and failed to replace William II on the throne with the Conqueror's older son, Robert, who had been awarded the then more important Normandy as his inheritance.

Rochester was a formidable place, as King John found out in 1215 when he personally led the onslaught there against his rebellious barons. The siege was a long and bitter one, and only ended when John's sappers undermined the south-east tower with tunnels held up by wooden props, which were then set on fire causing the collapse of the tower above them. Even then the defenders did not give up until they were starved out. The king was so furious at their defiance that he had to be deterred from having them all hanged.

The castle ghost dates from this episode – a white lady, said to be Lady Blanche de Warenne, who was killed by an arrow through her heart during the fighting. She has been seen many times, staggering along with the arrow still protruding from her chest. But there is also a more recent ghost – that of Charles Dickens who is said to haunt the moat on Christmas Eve: echoes of Marley's ghost, perhaps, in *A Christmas Carol*!

ABOVE *The pathetic cries of a baby still echo through the walls of Reculver.*

OPPOSITE *Rochester Castle, haunted by Lady Blanche and Charles Dickens.*

While yet a boy I sought for ghosts, and sped

Through many a listening chamber, cave and ruin

And starlight wood, with fearful steps pursuing

Hopes of high talk with the departed dead.

PERCY BYSSHE SHELLEY, 'HYMN TO INTELLECTUAL BEAUTY'

Hadleigh Castle

ESSEX

The ruins of this impressive 13th-century fortress inspired John Constable's memorable painting, and also quite a few ghost stories. A woman dressed in white is reputed to haunt the castle, along with a man in black who is meant to be the Devil himself. However, sightings of them have always been at their highest when smugglers were due to land their booty and locals wanted to discourage the revenue men. They seemed to have failed in this on one occasion because graffiti in the ruins suggest that the castle was used as an observation point by the excise men.

There is a long tradition of mysterious blue lights that have been seen near the castle. These may well have something to do with the smuggling activities, but they are also associated with a local man called James 'Cunning'

Murrell. He supposedly earned his nickname from the Anglo-Saxon word 'conyng' meaning knowledgeable, and knowledgeable he certainly was. He was regarded as a white witch, his reputation further enhanced by the fact that he was the seventh son of a seventh son, and he served the local area as cobbler, doctor, vet, chemist, fortune teller and curse-lifter. Murrell had moved to Hadleigh in 1810 after being apprenticed to a chemist still-man in London. The Essex country folk were unsophisticated, with many still having a strong belief in witchcraft, and so Murrell's undoubted abilities were regarded as nothing short of magic. He had a special mirror for looking into the future, a telescope to investigate the heavens and a useful charm that enabled him to tell if people were telling the truth or not. At night

Knebworth House

he would go out to gather herbs for his healing potions, and he always collected them at the castle ruins where he felt the astrological powers were strongest. Many people reported seeing him on these nocturnal excursions surrounded by bright blue lights. On one occasion the landlord of the Castle Inn spotted the lights and, assuming it was the excise men, rushed out to divert them away from the smugglers who were due in that night – but he only found Murrell looking up at the stars with his own collection of twinkling lights encircling him. When this famous man died in 1860 his box of magic was buried in his cottage garden, but his ghost is still reputed to haunt the place where he gathered his medicinal herbs. Cunning Murrell's silhouette has been seen by the castle ruins, surrounded by an aura of dancing blue lights.

This wonderful Gothic mansion is the ancestral home of the Lytton family – as well as several ghosts. The spirit of the famous Victorian politician and author, Edward Bulwer-Lytton, pervades the study and drawing room, which is hardly surprising as during his lifetime he had a great fascination for the occult and often held séances at Knebworth. He was the leading author of fantasy and

PAGE 76
Statue, Anglesey Abbey,
Cambridgeshire.

PAGE 77
Layer Marney Towers, Essex.

OPPOSITE *The ruins of*
Hadleigh Castle, the haunt of

smugglers and ghosts.

ABOVE *Knebworth House,*
ancestral home of the occult
writer Edward Bulwer-Lytton.

OVERLEAF *Bulwer-Lytton's*
study, which is still haunted by
his ghost.

science fiction of the time and his books had a profound influence on such writers as Charles Dickens, Wilkie Collins and Anthony Trollope. His work included the novel *Zanoni* and the acclaimed haunted-house story, *The Hunters and the Haunted or the House and the Brain*, and he also penned that well-known phrase, 'The pen is mightier than the sword.'

In the deep of night, the unmistakable sound of a spinning wheel has often been heard whirring away in the east wing of the house. Legend has it that the spectral spinner is the tormented ghost of a young girl who was imprisoned in that part of the house with only a spinning wheel for company. Known as Jenny Spinner, her crime had been to fall in love with a man of inferior birth. The cruel treatment broke her heart and her spirit, and finally the poor girl lost her mind. She died soon after, but her spirit seems doomed to continue the frantic spinning she did in her lifetime.

Another tragic ghost is that of a beautiful woman who haunts the Beauchamp chamber. A visitor to the house had a shock when he woke in the night to find a very upset woman in the room who kept pointing towards a section of the wall. She then disappeared as suddenly as she had arrived. Any lingering thought that he had merely experienced a particularly vivid nightmare vanished the next day when that part of the wall was examined. It proved to have a secret panel hiding a lock of hair and a phial of poison – clues perhaps to the lady's fate.

A ghost that predicts the fate of the person who encounters it has also been seen at Knebworth. The yellow or 'radiant' boy is a glowing spectre whose appearance foretells a rise to great power, but then a violent death. The last person he reputedly appeared to was Lord Castlereagh and the ghost drew its fingers across its throat. Castlereagh committed suicide in 1822 by cutting his throat with a penknife.

Orford Castle

SUFFOLK

Fishermen checking their nets off the Suffolk coast near Orford caught more than they bargained for when they discovered a merman tangled up with the more usual herrings. This was in the early 12th century when the small village had been transformed into an important seaport after Henry II built a unique castle there. The king was anxious to quell any rebellion from the barons of Norfolk and Suffolk, particularly the influential and discontented Bigod family.

The excited fishermen took their catch up to the castle where Bartholomew de Glanville was the castellan. He was thrilled with the strange, hairy creature, described as being just like a human being, and he decided to keep it as a novelty to enthral his guests. The merman was therefore given a room in the castle, but he proved to be very unsociable, keeping to his bed for much of the time and refusing to speak to anyone. Even when tortured and hung up by his feet, the merman would not utter a word, and when he was taken to church to see if that provoked a reaction, he horrified his captors by refusing to bow down to the sacred images he was shown. He did, however, have a prodigious appetite for raw fish which he would squeeze between his hands until absolutely dry and then eat whole. He also enjoyed swimming, which he was allowed to do as long as the fishermen had three lines of nets to keep him in. He soon escaped, however, by diving underneath the nets, but before long was bobbing up by the boats wanting more fish. As by this time his novelty value was wearing a little thin at the castle, the merman was allowed his freedom. He hung around for a little while before disappearing.

This fascinating story was recorded in about 1207 by the monk Ralph of Coggeshall in his *Chronicon Anglicanum*. However, it's rather sad to think that the so-called merman may well have been a seal!

Dunwich

SUFFOLK

It is not surprising that M R James, the celebrated author of ghost stories, based one of his most famous tales here. The windswept shoreline of Dunwich provided him with a perfect setting for his masterpiece of horror, *Whistle and I'll Come to You*. It is the sea that has sealed the fate of this isolated place, once the capital of East Anglia, as the waves have eaten away at the cliffs and swallowed the thriving town. It once had 52 churches, a bishop's palace, a mayor's mansion and vast ancient bronze gates. However, centuries of erosion and a great storm in 1328 mean that all that remains today are a few cottages, the ruins of a 13th-century Franciscan priory and an ancient leper hospital – all of which were originally more than a mile inland! Most of old Dunwich gradually toppled over the cliffs and now lies beneath the sea. All Saints was the last of the churches to succumb, finally falling in the early 20th century, but legend has it that the phantom bells of the old churches can still be heard tolling in the deep. Divers tend to avoid exploring the town's submerged ruins which have a sinister reputation, and shrouded figures seen on the clifftops are reputed to be the former inhabitants of Dunwich returning from their watery grave. Weird, distorted forms have been spotted near the 12th-century leper hospital and lights appear in the ruins of Greyfriars Priory. The woods near the priory are the haunt of the tormented spirit of a young man who searches through eternity trying to find his bride who jilted him for another lover.

Writing in the 19th century, the poet Algernon Charles Swinburne recalled the horrific effects of erosion at Dunwich as the brisk wind off the sea used to scour the graves in the churchyards to reveal the skeletons:

> *Tombs, with bare white piteous bones protruded,*
> *Shroudless, down the loose collapsing banks,*
> *Crumble, from their constant place detruded ...*

Now a solitary gravestone is all that remains in the churchyard of All Saints – a lonely reminder of the city under the sea.

OPPOSITE *Thetford Priory,*
where a ghostly Mass has been
heard amid the ruins.

Bury St Edmunds Abbey

SUFFOLK

The martyred remains of King Edmund were buried here in 903 and the site became an important place of pilgrimage. Later, the Benedictine abbey established here became one of the richest and most important in the country. In 1214 an historic meeting was held at the abbey between King John and his dissatisfied earls and barons, as a result of which Magna Carta was signed at Runnymede.

Although the abbey was a place of such prestige and power, it did not have a happy relationship with the town. By the 14th century the situation hit an all-time low and there were riots against the wealth of the abbots, which resulted in considerable damage to the abbey and the death of several monks. The ghosts of monks have been reported near the abbey gates and in the cellars of buildings in Abbeygate Street. Two grey ladies have also been spotted. One, it is claimed, is the spirit of Maude Carew who took part in a plot to assassinate the Duke of Gloucester, brother of Henry VII. She was meant to administer poison to him but somehow ended up drinking the poison herself.

After the Dissolution of the Monasteries, most of the abbey buildings fell into ruin. The important role it had played in English history seemed forgotten by the 18th century as the *Annual Register* for 1772 records:

February 18th. Some workmen who were employed in the ruins of the Abbey at St Edmund's Bury, found a leaden coffin, made after the ancient custom, exactly the shape of the body. This had been enclosed in an oak case, which, by length of time, was decayed, but the lead remained perfect. Upon closer examination, it was found to be the body of Thomas Beaufort, Duke of Exeter, uncle to Henry V and deposited in 1427. On opening the lead, the flesh, hair, and toe and hand nails, were as perfect and sound as though he had not been dead six hours.

A surgeon in the neighbourhood made an incision in the breast, and declared the flesh cut as firm as in a living subject, and there was even an appearance of blood; multitudes of people were present and saw the same. At this time the corpse was not in the least noisome, but being exposed to the air, it presently became putrid and offensive. The workmen coming early Friday morning, resolved to make a prize of the lead, and therefore cut out the corpse, tumbled it into a hole near at hand, and threw dirt on it. The lead was conveyed directly to the plumbers, and there sold for twenty-two shillings. Thus, in Shakespeare's phrase, was 'a great man knocked about the sconce with a dirty shovel'.

Thetford Priory

NORFOLK

The Priory of Our Lady of Thetford was founded in the early 12th century as home to a community of Canons of the Holy Sepulchre. The ruins are now the only standing remains in England of this small independent religious order. In the 13th century, local people claimed to have seen a vision of the Virgin Mary who asked them to build a chapel in her honour. During the construction work on the Lady Chapel, an old statue of the Virgin Mary was discovered and inside the hollow head were the relics of saints. As a result the priory became a place of pilgrimage and miraculous cures were reported.

A ghostly Mass has been heard in the ruins, with singing in Latin followed by a reading from a text. Monks have been spotted drifting around the grounds, and a nearby hotel, formerly part of the priory, has a long-term guest in the shape of a phantom monk.

Burgh Castle

NORFOLK

An assortment of ghostly phenomena surround this vast Roman fort, formerly known as Gariannonum and part of a string of forts along what the Romans called the Saxon Shore. A spectral fleet has been seen and heard making its way to the castle, and the feared black dog known in Norfolk as a 'shuck' has also been sighted. With blood-red eyes and enormous fangs, these hell-hounds appear in many different parts of the country and have their own regional names. An ancient battle in which the Danes massacred the Saxon army is also reputedly rerun at certain times. Then, every 3 July, a figure wrapped in a white flag is hurled from the castle ramparts and rolls down to the foreshore. And as if that wasn't already enough, there's also the mischievous spirit of Baron Rudolph Scarfe, who lived near the castle and who now apparently delights in tricking and teasing his victims.

Blickling Hall

NORFOLK

This red-brick Jacobean mansion was built on the site of an earlier house – one owned by the Boleyn family who rose to prominence at the Tudor Court after Anne Boleyn became the second wife of King Henry VIII. Her charms quickly dimmed when she gave birth to a daughter, Elizabeth, rather than the longed-for male heir to the throne, and her fate was sealed when Jane Seymour took Henry's fickle fancy.

Anne was reputedly born at Blickling Hall and spent many happy childhood years there – as she wistfully recalled when she was imprisoned in the Tower of London. As she awaited execution after being found guilty of a trumped-up charge of treason and adultery with five men, including her own brother, Lord Rochford, she wrote:

> *A captive, I in this dread Tower, scenes of childhood*
> *gaiety recall,*
> *They comfort bring in this dark hour, now gaiety*
> *hath flown …*
> *Oh, were I still a child in stature small*
> *To tread the rose-lined paths of Blickling Hall.*

ABOVE *A ghostly black dog with blood-red eyes reputedly frequents the Roman fort of Burgh Castle.*
OPPOSITE *A statue in the gardens of Blickling Hall.*

And it seems that she does indeed tread the paths again as her ghost reputedly returns to Blickling Hall every 19 May, the anniversary of her execution in 1536. Just before midnight a phantom coach sweeps up the drive pulled by four headless horses and driven by a headless coachman. It stops as it reaches the front door and out steps Anne Boleyn, carrying her severed head. The coach then disappears, but Anne remains to walk around her beloved childhood home until cockcrow heralds the dawn.

Many people have reported seeing her ghost (both with and without her head). All the descriptions tally – she is dressed in a long grey dress with a white lace collar and wears a white cap. And there was a strange and spine-tingling incident when a large painting of Anne's daughter, Queen Elizabeth I, was taken away for cleaning. The carriers who were returning the painting to Blickling after the necessary work had been done were held up,

and finally arrived late at night when only two members of staff remained at the Hall. The two staff waited in the entrance lobby while the painting was taken by the carriers into the dining room where it would be redisplayed. When the men returned they were asked if they needed a signature for the delivery of the painting. That wasn't necessary, they explained, because the lady in the dining room had signed for it. But there was no lady in the dining room! And when the delivery note was examined there was no signature either. It was only then that the two staff members realised that it was 19 May!

The ghost of Anne's father, Sir Thomas Boleyn, also makes an annual reappearance. Afraid to lose his position at Court, he betrayed both Anne and her brother and so was held partly responsible for their violent deaths on the block. As a penance, his restless spirit is doomed to appear on the anniversary of his death in 1539 driving a coach over 12 bridges around Blickling Hall before dawn. The apparition apparently travels at breakneck speed around the countryside pursued by a pack of howling demons, and will continue to do so until 1,000 years have passed since his death.

The airmen of Bircham Newton

Many of the ghosts in the lovely, misty and haunted county of Norfolk are those of young men, their spirits seemingly returning to continue their duties and to find comfort in the place they regard as home. During the Second World War the county was peppered with RAF stations, the home and place of duty of so many of the brave young airmen of the 1940s.

The strange phenomena at RAF Bircham Newton have been well documented, and the airfield has long had a reputation for being haunted. During the 1940s, people sleeping in the Officers' Mess experienced the terrifying feeling that they were being smothered by a heavy weight, and something that looked like a huge black stain was seen by two officers. Subsequent investigation revealed that a young wartime pilot, suffering severe stress and feeling he was losing his nerve, had shot himself in that room, and his blood had stained the floor. The room was sealed and never used as accommodation again.

In the 1970s there was a great deal of interest in the paranormal activity centred in the old squash courts. Several people experienced 'cold spots' when they were in the building, and there was the unmistakable sound of someone walking along the viewing gallery, even when the doors were locked. A player who was practising one night had the feeling that he was being watched from the gallery. Glancing up, he was surprised to see an RAF pilot in a Second World War flying jacket, looking down at him. Eventually, two men decided to lock themselves in the courts overnight with a tape recorder, but they lost their nerve and bolted when, in the middle of the night, the sound of footsteps came from the gallery. However, the tape continued recording, and when it was played everyone was stunned to hear clanks, bangs and voices – the sounds of a busy wartime hangar. There was the drone of an aircraft and a woman's voice shouting something, but the background noise was too great to make out the words. The tape was examined carefully, but there was nothing wrong with it, and subsequent recordings revealed similar noises.

A BBC film crew visiting the airfield later saw two airmen, dressed in Sidcot jackets, flying helmets and boots walk into the old squash courts and then disappear inside. Rumour has it that the ghostly airmen are the spirits of the pilot and crew members of an Avro Anson that crashed near the airfield perimeter during the war. They were all close friends – and keen squash players.

Blakeney Guildhall

NORFOLK

In the 15th century, Blakeney was the third most important port in Norfolk. Originally probably built as the house of a wealthy merchant, the building became the Guildhall, and by 1516 was being used by the town's guild of fish merchants. The fine vaulted basement or undercroft was put to a host of different uses in later years including coal storage and as a temporary mortuary for shipwrecked sailors during the First World War. One of Blakeney's many tunnels is reputed to be situated here, giving access to Baconthorpe Castle. It is also claimed that there is a whole network of tunnels under the town and that the

Carmelite friary at Blakeney and Wiverton Hall are also linked to the Guildhall. These may have been useful for moving contraband goods around the town as Blakeney was quite a haunt of smugglers.

Here too there is the frequently told story of a fiddler exploring the tunnel at the Guildhall, never to be seen again (see also Binham Priory and Rushton Triangular Lodge). Its importance to the town is shown by the fact that a figure of a fiddler is carved into Blakeney's attractive sign.

Binham Priory

NORFOLK

As you would expect, the ghost of a monk is reputed to haunt this 11th-century Benedictine priory. The legend of the Black Monk has been well known for centuries, as has another folk tale about a tunnel linking the priory with Walsingham Abbey, some miles away. One day, it is said, a travelling fiddler boasted to local people that he would go down the tunnel to see where it went, and whether the Black Monk lurked down there. So, accompanied by his faithful little dog, he set off into the tunnel, playing his violin as he went so that the villagers could track his progress from above the ground. The playing merrily continued until a nearby hill was reached. Suddenly, it stopped. The villagers waited, expecting to hear it again on the far side of the hill, but there was only silence until the fiddler's terrified dog came streaking out of the tunnel's entrance. The poor fiddler was never found, and the hill he disappeared under was forever after known as Fiddler's Hill. In 1933 road-widening work cut into the hill which was found to be an ancient barrow. Three skeletons were found, including one of a dog.

OPPOSITE *The eerie ruin of Binham Priory, haunted by the shadows of a black monk and a tragic fiddler.*

Castle Rising Castle

NORFOLK

On wild, wet nights unearthly howls and screams have been heard at the top of this 12th-century castle. They are said to come from the tormented spirit of Queen Isabella, wife of Edward II, who was nicknamed the 'She-Wolf of France'. Some say that her spirit is still drawn to the place where she was imprisoned for 27 years for her part in the murder of her husband.

Isabella's marriage was doomed from the start as Edward much preferred the company of his own sex, and his favourite Piers Gaveston in particular. Isabella took a lover, Roger Mortimer, and the two plotted the downfall of the king. Mortimer raised a successful revolt and Edward was imprisoned and brutally murdered in Berkeley Castle, Gloucestershire. But when his son, Edward III, came of age, he avenged his father's death by ordering the execution of Mortimer and the imprisonment of his mother. It wasn't too unpleasant for Isabella, however, as she was granted privileges and servants, and was allowed to move from place to place. She was not supposed to show her face in public and so, in order to worship, she had a tunnel built linking Castle Rising Castle with the Red Mount Chapel at King's Lynn. Eventually, Isabella lost her mind and her insane cries apparently still reverberate round the castle. Some people claim she lives up to her name by actually returning in the form of a huge white wolf that has red eyes, blood dripping from its fangs and a howl to wake the dead.

OPPOSITE *Castle Rising Castle, where the ghostly manic screams of the 'She Wolf of France' are still heard some 600 years after her death.*

Night's swift dragons cut the clouds full fast,

And yonder shines Aurora's harbinger;

At whose approach, ghosts, wandering here and there,

Troop home to churchyards.

WILLIAM SHAKESPEARE, 'A MIDSUMMER NIGHT'S DREAM'

The Icknield Way

OXFORDSHIRE

This prehistoric road, winding its way across the middle of Britain from Norfolk to Buckinghamshire, was old when the Romans arrived and can claim to be the oldest road in Britain. Parts of it were reputed, by those who lived near it in centuries past, to lead to the end of the world.

It is haunted by many ghosts along the length of its route, including Roman legionaries, black dogs and phantom coaches. Boudicca's charioteers have also been seen, careering madly along the Way towards St Albans which they sacked in AD 61.

Rycote Chapel

OXFORDSHIRE

Taking its name from the cornfields it was set in, Rycote Park was once a magnificent mansion visited by Henry VIII, Elizabeth I, James I and Charles I. It was destroyed by fire in 1745 and only the stable block and chapel were left unscathed. The chapel was built in the 15th century and there are many stories associated with it: eerie encounters with monks, a 17th-century milkmaid and even Sir Thomas More, reportedly recognised by a visitor to the chapel, though it is not clear how he was identified. The most persistent presence seems to be a grey lady, known affectionately to the staff there as Arabella, who haunts the chapel on moonlit nights.

PREVIOUS PAGE LEFT *Sculpture on Moreton Corbet Castle.*
PREVIOUS PAGE RIGHT *Wood carving on the gatehouse of Stokesay Castle.*
OPPOSITE *Part of the Icknield Way, a prehistoric track believed to lead to the end of the world.*

She is sometimes seen in broad daylight too. There is a very detailed account of a sighting of Arabella, written and published by the custodian of the time. It took place at precisely 3.55pm on 4 December 1968 – the afternoon of the night of the full moon. He first caught sight of her standing by the ancient yew tree that was said to have been planted to mark the coronation of King Stephen in 1135. His first thought was that it must be someone in fancy dress as her costume was in the Tudor style with square neck, tight waist, full skirt and voluminous sleeves. The soft grey material shimmered like satin and he could clearly make out the intricate embroidery and jewelled decoration. The lady was tall and slim but her face was turned away and obscured by the flowing veil of her tightly fitting circular headdress. As he walked towards her she vanished behind the yew, but there was no one there when he got to the tree. Looking around, he spotted her again moving across the grass by the eastern end of the chapel. Feeling no fear, the custodian followed her and described how she glided rather than walked along by the north side of the building, paused facing the double doors and then moved quickly towards the site of Rycote Park, following the route used in former days from the chapel to the great house. She passed beneath the chestnut tree, down the slope and, as she reached the level grass at the bottom, just disappeared. The custodian was then conscious of an icy feeling and found that he was trembling uncontrollably.

Minster Lovell Hall

OXFORDSHIRE

This 15th-century manor house was once the home of one of Richard III's closest allies, Francis, Viscount Lovell. He held positions of enormous power in the country and fought with Richard at Bosworth Field in 1485. After the battle he managed to escape to Flanders but returned to take part in Lambert Simnel's rebellion of 1487. Although reputedly killed at the Battle of Stoke in 1487, there were strong rumours, later reported by the writer Francis Bacon, that Lovell had escaped after the battle with a price on his head and gone into hiding in an underground vault in his manor house. The rumour was that his

OPPOSITE *Minster Lovell Hall, the setting for the tragic tale of the bride locked in an oaken chest.*

presence was known only to an elderly servant, who kept him securely locked away and brought him food. When the servant died suddenly Lovell was trapped and starved to death.

In 1708, when footings were being dug for a new chimney at Minster Lovell, the builders broke through into a large underground room. It is reported that a skeleton sat at a table in this room, a book, paper and pen in front of him, with the remains of his faithful dog lying at his feet. His ghost is said to haunt the ruins.

Minster Lovell appears to have attracted tragedy. One Christmas at the Hall young William Lovell celebrated his wedding to his beautiful bride. The guests decided on a game of hide-and-seek, but when it was the bride's turn to hide, no-one could find her. The distraught bridegroom and the guests searched for days, but she was never found. Years later, servants clearing out the attic opened a heavy old oak chest, and found inside it a skeleton dressed in a bridal gown. The heavy lid had fallen and locked her inside. On windy winter nights the mournful cries of William can be heard as he searches for his lost bride. The Victorian ballad 'The Mistletoe Bough' (1884) by Thomas Haynes Bayly celebrates this story:

> *They sought her that night! And they sought her*
> *next day!*
> *And they sought her in vain when a week pass'd away!*
> *In the highest – the lowest – the loneliest spot,*
> *Young Lovell sought wildly – but found her not.*
>
> *And years flew by, and their grief at last*
> *Was told as a sorrowful tale long past;*
> *And when Lovell appeared, the children cried*
> *'See! The old man weeps for his fairy bride.'*

> *At length an old chest, that had long laid hid,*
> *Was found in the castle – they raised the lid –*
> *And a skeleton form lay mouldering there,*
> *In the bridal wreath of that lady fair.*
>
> *Oh! Sad was her fate! – in sportive jest*
> *She hid from her lord in the old oak chest.*
> *It closed with a spring! – and, dreadful doom,*
> *The bride lay clasp'd in her living tomb!*

A curious coda to the tale of the Lovell bride trapped forever in a heavy chest is that there is an ancient wooden chest kept in the church at Terrington St Clement in Norfolk – where there is also a 'Lovell pew' – that is said to have held the skeleton of a bride. She is said to emerge from her coffin once a year to join the choir in their singing.

The Rollright Stones

OXFORDSHIRE

The Rollright Stones consist of three Neolithic monuments close to each other. The King Stone is a solitary standing stone, the Whispering Knights are the remains of the burial chamber of a long barrow and the King's Men is a perfect circle of standing stones. They get their names from the legend of their formation, when a witch met a Danish king and his men who were seeking to conquer England. She turned them all into stone and herself into an elder tree. The Whispering Knights look like a group of figures leaning conspiratorially towards each other, possibly plotting against the king, who stands in solitary splendour while his soldiers form their circle nearby.

There are many legends associated with the Stones. It is said that at midnight the King's Men come alive, join hands and dance in a circle. They then go down to drink at a spring in Little Rollright spinney. Witnesses to these events will go mad or die. It is also perilous to chip away at the stones. A man from Banbury took a chipping, and when he returned to his cart he found that the wheels had locked solid and he could not move. And a young soldier took a piece with him to India as a good luck charm; but it did him no good – he fell ill and died of typhus as soon as he arrived. The elder tree has its own tale. It is said to form part of a hedge between the King Stone and the King's Men, and to bleed when cut. On Midsummer's Eve people used to gather round the King Stone, which was seen to move its head when the elder was cut.

There was once a farmer who decided to remove the capstone of the Whispering Knights to make a bridge over a stream. It took 20 horses to drag the stone down the hill, and two men died in the process. Once laid in place the stone gave him no peace: he continually heard weird noises and every morning he would find that the stone had turned over and repositioned itself on the bank of the stream. When he gave in and returned it to its rightful place it took a single horse to drag it easily up the hill.

As with many stone circles, it is claimed that the stones can never be counted twice with the same result. A baker tried to do it, by baking a number of loaves and placing one on each stone. But whenever he tried to count the loaves he would find that some had moved or disappeared – spirited away by the Devil, or the fairies who are said to live in caves under the stones and to come out at midnight and dance by the light of the moon. A stone placed over the entrance to these caves will be found in the morning to have turned over.

It seems that the power of this place is no illusion, as our own photographer can reveal (see Foreword).

Hailes Abbey
GLOUCESTERSHIRE

This late Cistercian abbey was founded in the mid-13th century by Richard, Earl of Cornwall, to give thanks for his safe delivery from a shipwreck at sea. Only a few years after its foundation, the abbey was extended to provide a suitable home for a phial of holy blood, said to be some of the actual blood that flowed from Christ's side as he died on the cross and was collected in the Holy Grail – a link to another major religious mystery that did Hailes no harm! The blood reputedly never congealed, and it was claimed that only the truly holy could see it in its sacred phial. Sceptics dismissed it as the blood of a duck, constantly renewed!

As a result of its possession of this major relic, Hailes became a great centre of pilgrimage and accumulated vast riches – no doubt fuelled by the gullible pilgrims who paid through the nose for the Masses and indulgences that would make them holy enough to actually see the blood. The assumption is that they were shown an empty phial until the shrewd monks reckoned that they had bled them enough; and only then was the sleight of hand performed that allowed them to see the real thing. Henry VIII's commissioners were not to be beguiled, however; they dismissed the blood as fake, destroyed the relic and bestowed the abbey on Katherine Parr, the king's sixth – and surviving – wife, who lived in nearby Sudeley Castle in Winchcombe.

This does not apparently prevent the monkish guardians of the blood revisiting their old home and continuing to carry out the duties that were theirs when the abbey was a fully functioning centre of worship and pilgrimage. Local people avoid it on moonless nights.

Goodrich Castle

HEREFORDSHIRE

Superbly positioned high above the River Wye, Goodrich Castle commanded an important crossing point between England and Wales. The small 12th-century keep still stands three storeys high, offering superb views over the countryside around; but at its foot is a nasty little dungeon, narrow and windowless. The stone door-frame still exhibits the square holes for the bar that was slid across the front of the door to stop it being opened. Usually such holes are on the inside of the door to keep people out; here, of course, they are on the outside since their purpose was to keep people in.

The Welsh Marches were a turbulent part of the world during most of the Middle Ages, and Goodrich was one of a chain of 'Marcher' castles along the border aimed at controlling this volatile region. But it only really saw

major action during the Civil War when its Royalist garrison was besieged for three months in 1646 by Colonel Birch. And it was then that the legend of Goodrich was born…

The story is one of tragic lovers: Alice, Colonel Birch's niece, had fallen in love with a Royalist, Charles Clifford, and was with him in Goodrich Castle when her uncle placed it under siege. Fearing for their lives, they tried to escape under the cover of a violent storm one night. But they had not reckoned on how swollen the river had become, and they were swept away to their deaths.

Their spirits are said to haunt the castle, particularly during stormy weather when their shrieks can be heard from the river. A ghostly horseman with a woman riding behind him has been spotted at the foot of the walls by the river, vainly trying to urge his horse on, and a 'white lady' has also been seen.

Wigmore Castle

This 'Marcher' castle was one of the greatest strongholds of the Mortimers, powerful lords who sometimes meddled with the kings and suffered for it. One of them, Roger Mortimer, was the lover of Edward II's wife, Isabella – the 'She-Wolf of France' – and was complicit with her in the grisly murder of her husband at Berkeley Castle. Perhaps in revenge for his preference for his favourite, Piers Gaveston, Edward was reputedly killed by a red-hot skewer inserted into his entrails. When his son, Edward III, became old enough to avenge his father, he imprisoned his mother at Castle Rising – which she still haunts – and awarded Mortimer the shame of a common felon's death by hanging at Tyburn.

Wigmore Castle is now a tranquil ruin, still covered with the vegetation of centuries and recently protected by a programme of removing the plants and the undergrowth, conserving the masonry beneath and replacing the foliage. But the misdeeds of its former lords live on in a story about a bridge over the River Dee, further up the Welsh border. One of the Mortimers was appointed, with John, Earl Warren, guardian of the two young orphaned sons of Madog ap Gruffydd of Dinas Bran. But they were greedy for the wealth that the two boys would inherit, and one freezing night they brought them on horseback from Chester, and when they reached the bridge at Holt, plucked them from their mounts and heaved them into the icy river. They looked on grimly as the boys screamed for help, and stone-heartedly waited until they drowned. The cries of the two boys are still to be heard under the bridge.

Stokesay Castle

SHROPSHIRE

This fortified manor house on the Welsh Marches was built in the 13th century by Lawrence of Ludlow, the leading wool merchant of the time. It is a remarkably well-preserved survival, combining a comfortable residence with strong defences, which on that troubled border were probably still advisable even though Edward I had recently defeated the Welsh prince Llewelyn.

It is said that, once upon a time, two giant brothers lived above Stokesay Castle, one on View Edge and the other at Norton Camp. They shared their vast wealth and kept it in a strong oak chest in the vaults at Stokesay Castle. The problem was that there was only one key to the chest, so whichever brother had the key would throw it to the other when it was needed. But one day, one of the brothers threw it short and it landed in the castle moat.

They searched for it long and hard, but the key had disappeared deep into the mud where it reputedly still lies today. The treasure chest, too, sits in the vaults at Stokesay, guarded by a giant raven who will allow it to be opened only when the key is found. As for the brothers, they died of sadness at losing their treasure and are said to wander the hills around Stokesay, still searching mournfully for the lost key.

OPPOSITE *Wood carving on the gatehouse of Stokesay Castle.*
ABOVE *Stokesay Castle, where a giant raven guards a lost treasure.*

This Spectred Isle The Midlands

Wenlock Priory

SHROPSHIRE

The torture and gruesome murder of a nun have left their imprint on this large Cluniac priory. The story, however, relates not to the Norman chapter house and 13th-century church that remain today, but back to the monastery founded here shortly before AD 690 by Merewald, a member of the royal house of the Kingdom of Mercia. It was a double house: primarily a nunnery but served by priests who also lived a religious life. The first abbess was St Milburga, daughter of Merewald, who was said to have power over birds and be able to levitate. The macabre death of a nun in 874 at the hands of the Danes has never been explained: she was raped, dragged behind a horse and garrotted by twisting an axe in the rope around her neck. One wonders what she had done to deserve such a gruesome end, and her ghost has been seen stalking the place where she suffered so cruelly.

Moreton Corbet Castle

SHROPSHIRE

The ruins of this medieval castle and the partly-built Elizabethan manor house that replaced part of it are both picturesque and eerie. Moreover, it is said both to be cursed and to be haunted by the aggrieved neighbour who cursed it. A Jacobean Corbet upset his neighbour, Paul Homeyard, by refusing to help him when he needed it, and had his house and himself roundly cursed in return. Homeyard foretold that the house would never be finished, and he returned after death to haunt it, wandering forlornly around its ruined walls on moonlit nights.

OPPOSITE *The Elizabethan ruin of Moreton Corbet Castle is both cursed and haunted.*

Lilleshall Abbey

SHROPSHIRE

The hauntings at the ruins of this Augustinian abbey may date from its use as an abbey proper or from the time during the Civil War when it became a fortified stronghold. The elderly, black-robed monkish figure who accosted a former custodian and spoke to him before vanishing clearly belongs to the earlier history of the place, but the shrieks and cries emanating from the ruins in the early evening are more likely to relate to its later use. Its setting in the midst of lawns and elderly yew trees only adds to its tranquil mysteriousness.

Beeston Castle

CHESHIRE

Known as the Castle of the Rock, Beeston enjoys perhaps the most dramatic position of any castle in England. Its long history dates back to the Bronze Age when a fortress was built on the cliff-top, but the present castle dates from the 13th century when the Earl of Chester owned it. He had been fighting in the Crusades where the impressive Syrian defences influenced his plans for the redesign of Beeston. On his return home, he put these revolutionary new designs into action and Beeston soon began to look very like the fortress at Sahyoun. The castle later passed into the hands of the crown, and legend has it that Richard II hid a vast fortune here in 1399. His treasure trove was reportedly secreted here as a precaution before he went off to Ireland, but on his return to England he was captured and killed and never had the chance to retrieve it.

The castle has one of the nicest ghosts in the country. She is a pretty lady dressed in a lacy white dress and she appears only to children. She is seen walking across the outer bailey of the castle and turns her head over her shoulder to smile. She brings an aura of kindness with her, and centuries ago must have enjoyed some very happy association with Beeston Castle.

Many visitors to the castle have reported that their dogs are afraid to go into certain areas. A custodian recently took a friend's dog with her while she checked round the castle when all the visitors had left but, as she came to the West Tower in the inner bailey, he stopped and refused to go any further. She tried to coax him forward but he just stood there staring ahead, making strange noises and growling deep in his throat. Something that only he could see in the West Tower was a threat – and he was not prepared to face it.

When a well-known clairvoyant visited the castle he was asked if he had seen or felt anything. He said that he had not encountered anything really sinister, but had experienced a couple of flashbacks in time to the medieval period. He had witnessed a woman soaking her feet in the outer bailey, and someone being pushed down the castle well – which may account for the frequent reports of a low moaning being heard issuing from the well.

Peveril Castle

DERBYSHIRE

William Peveril had quite an influence in this part of the country as, in addition to Bolsover, he also built this castle, known as the Castle of the Peak. Clinging to a steep rocky outcrop, it provided Sir Walter Scott with the inspiration for his famous novel *Peveril of the Peak*. Perhaps Scott also knew about one of the castle's ghosts – a knight in clanking armour who stalks the keep while his phantom horse waits below. Weird blue lights sometimes illuminate the castle at night and an evil 'shuck' pads about the precincts. These phantom black dogs are reported in all parts of the country and have different local names. Whatever they are called, however, their appearance means the same thing. Bad luck.

Wingfield Manor

With its late Gothic Great Hall and magnificent high tower, Wingfield Manor seems a natural place to find supernatural phenomena. And there are many to find. Perhaps the most famous is the ghost of Mary, Queen of Scots, one of the most active apparitions in the country, who haunts the ruins at certain times of the year. When she was alive, she couldn't wait to leave the place where she had been imprisoned on the orders of Queen Elizabeth I, and complained bitterly about her dark and smelly accommodation.

Wingfield Manor was one of the largest courtyard palaces in England when it was built in the 15th century, and a testament to the wealth and power of its owner, Lord Cromwell, Treasurer to Henry VI. By the reign of Elizabeth I, the house was owned by the Earls of Shrewsbury, and it was the sixth Earl who was ordered by the queen to keep Mary under lock and key. Her imprisonment must have been quite lax because it is said that Sir Anthony Babington used to steal into the house under cover of dark to plot her escape and the downfall of Elizabeth. He blackened his face with walnut juice so that he could pass as a 'common' man, and carried a few nuts in his pocket for the purpose. Legend has it that one night a walnut fell from his pocket and grew into the magnificent tree in the courtyard. The present tree is nearly 300 years old and grows from the stump of a much earlier one. However, if another legend is to be believed, he had no need to resort to these tactics as he had had a tunnel built from the Babington family home at Dethwick to Wingfield Manor. This must have been some engineering feat as it had to drop through sandstone and under the river. There is no trace of it today. However, a tunnel has been discovered nearby at the Peacock at

OPPOSITE *Wingfield Manor, said to have been abandoned because of its many ghosts.*

Oakerthorpe; but this may have had more to do with avoiding the excise men. The legend may gain some credence from the numerous sunken drovers' roads that criss-cross this part of the country. When overgrown with trees, these green roads look very much like tunnels.

Many people have reported seeing strange blue lights flickering in the undercroft and there is also an intriguing murder mystery known as 'The Curse of Wingfield Manor'. When some old papers were recently discovered in the manor, they told the tale of a local girl named Mary who went to work as a maid there in 1666. Mary was in love with a young farmer, and she made the fatal mistake of revealing her passion to Fanny, another maid from the village. Mary had no idea that Fanny was in love with the same man and had hopes of becoming his wife. Mary arranged to go home to get consent from her family for the wedding but she never arrived. Her fate was not discovered until some years later when, on her deathbed, Fanny confessed that she had lured Mary into the dim recesses of the undercroft and locked her in. Sure enough, when this was investigated, Mary's skeleton was discovered huddled at the top of the steps behind the locked door. Whatever the truth of the story, ghostly activity is meant to be the reason why the manor was left uninhabited and finally fell into ruins.

Bolsover Castle

DERBYSHIRE

Situated in a fine defensive position on a hilltop, the original castle was built soon after the Norman Conquest by William Peveril, one of William the Conqueror's most loyal supporters. However, by the 17th century, defence was not a priority for the new owner – Sir Charles Cavendish, whose family owned Chatsworth House. What was important were the magnificent views and

OPPOSITE *High on a hill, the imposing façade of Bolsover Castle looms over the Derbyshire countryside.*

the fact that the neighbours were the Leakes of Sutton Hall (later Sutton Scarsdale) and his relative, Bess of Hardwick. Cavendish immediately started to redesign Bolsover in keeping with the fashion of the Romantic Age. He built the fascinating Little Castle as an elegant retreat – a place for recreation, repose and extravagant pleasure where he and his friends could imagine they were part of the golden age of chivalry. His son continued the lavish building programme, creating the fabulous Riding House where he could develop his skill as a horseman by practising the art of manège – where the horses perform elaborate balletic movements like the famous Lipizzaner stallions of the Spanish Riding School in Vienna.

It is in the domestic quarters, however, that a ghost has been reported. There seems to be a sad story behind the spectral figure of a woman who is regularly seen in the kitchen carrying a baby or small child wrapped in a shawl. She obviously cares deeply about the child because she very carefully lays it down before disappearing. But, inexplicably, she puts it in the fireplace!

A local legend claims that the Devil happened to be in Bolsover one day and was so impressed by the skills of the local blacksmith that he demanded to have metal shoes put on his hooves. Whether from fear or on purpose, the blacksmith drove a nail deep into the soft part of the Devil's hoof. With a great scream of agony, the Devil took off over the Derbyshire countryside, writhing and kicking with pain. The nearby church at Chesterfield was in his way and so felt the full force of one of the Devil's frenzied kicks – which accounts for the twisted spire!

Hardwick Old Hall

DERBYSHIRE

Bess of Hardwick was a remarkable woman. Born into a relatively poor family, she became the second richest woman in the kingdom after Elizabeth I. Through her four marriages and her own intellect and determination, she rose to a position of great power – despite being thrown into the Tower of London a couple of times when her actions displeased the queen! She married into the influential Cavendish family and later became the wife of George Talbot, sixth Earl of Shrewsbury, whose estates included Wingfield Manor and Rufford Abbey. However, it is not a ghost of the remarkable Bess who haunts her birthplace and family home, but that of Thomas Hobbes, the brilliant philosopher, mathematician and writer, who was companion and tutor to the Cavendish family for many years. He died at Hardwick in 1679. There are also stories from people claiming to have seen a monk in the grounds – this time without the usual hood hiding his face. Witnesses have all remarked on the shining white featureless face of this apparition.

Sutton Scarsdale Hall

DERBYSHIRE

Although the elaborate panelling that once graced this Georgian mansion is now to be found in museums in Philadelphia and Los Angeles, it is still possible to appreciate the house's former splendour. Home of the Leke (or Leake) family for several hundred years, the Hall is an 18th-century remodelling of an earlier house. The ghost of a sobbing white lady glides between the Hall and the nearby St Mary's Church.

Family legend recounts the romantic story of Sir Nicholas Leke. He was summoned to the Crusades and, before leaving, he broke a ring in two, keeping one half and giving the other to his wife as a sign of love and loyalty. Captured in the fighting and incarcerated for many years in prison, he kept himself going by thinking constantly about his wife and praying to be reunited with her. One night, as he prayed, he felt himself being swept up in a rushing wind which finally dropped him outside

the church door near his home. No-one would come near the strange, filthy figure who beseeched them for aid, until finally a good Samaritan went to help him. Nicholas proffered the broken ring and insisted that it should be taken up to the Hall and given to Lady Leke. Soon a grey-haired stranger came rushing down the church path towards him and it was only when she enfolded him in her arms that he recognised his long-lost love.

Another Sir Nicholas, who lived in Elizabethan times, left a dole to the poor of the parish in his will. The loaves were all to be stamped with the letter N and they had to be distributed every year. One year the dole was forgotten and a large well in the estate suddenly overflowed, causing widespread floods and crop damage. The bread loaves were quickly baked and handed out and the well water instantly went down.

A later member of the family was a staunch Royalist during the Civil War and he fortified the Hall against the Parliamentarian forces, but was forced out. He was reputedly so depressed by the execution of the king in 1649 that he had his grave dug in the grounds of the Hall and, every Friday, dressed himself in sackcloth and went and lay in the grave to contemplate the vagaries of human fortune.

ABOVE *The eerie ruin of Sutton Scarsdale Hall where a sobbing white lady is often seen.*

Rushton Triangular Lodge

NORTHAMPTONSHIRE

Built towards the end of the reign of Elizabeth I, this lodge is an affirmation of the Catholic faith of its builder, Sir Thomas Tresham. In a celebration of the Holy Trinity, everything about it is in threes: it is three storeys high, with three walls each with three windows, with three gables on top and a three-sided chimney. But its ghost takes a normal human form, as a phantom fiddler whose music has been heard coming from the lodge. As legend has it, the then owner of the lodge offered a large sum of money to anyone who would investigate the recently discovered secret passage underneath the building. A gypsy fiddler accepted the challenge and descended into the passage, playing his fiddle as he went. Listeners continued to hear the music for a while, but then it suddenly stopped. When the passage was cautiously investigated it was found to have collapsed and there was no sign of the fiddler, who was never seen again.

Fiddlers and drummer boys disappearing underground are a recurring theme: Blakeney Guildhall, Binham Priory and Richmond Castle have similar stories arising from the enduring fascination of secret tunnels.

Rufford Abbey

NOTTINGHAMSHIRE

This Cistercian monastery became the home of the Talbot family after the Dissolution, but in the early 17th century it passed to the Saviles who lived there until 1938. It has many ghosts, notably a White Lady who has often been seen gliding through the ruins or between the trees, and also a 'Little Old Lady in Black' who haunts the magnificent park around the abbey ruins.

More sinister is the 'Black Friar', a huge ghostly monk with a skull instead of a face under its cowl, who taps people on the shoulder or appears behind them reflected in a mirror. It is an encounter with this ghastly apparition that is recorded in the burial register of a church nearby as causing the death of a local man in the early 20th century.

A poignant story concerns the tale of a terrified child who was pursued through the corridors at Rufford and tried to hide in one of the four-poster beds but was caught and murdered. Several guests of the Saviles in later centuries were awakened by what seemed to be a shivering child nestling up to them in bed and clearly seeking comfort and safety. No real child was ever discovered.

OPPOSITE *Rushton Triangular Lodge, built in celebration of the Holy Trinity, and the haunt of a phantom fiddler.*
RIGHT *A sculpture at Rufford Abbey, where a skeletal Black Friar roams the dark corridors.*

The Dambusters

The fertile fields of Lincolnshire, unobstructed by mountains, were the perfect sites for Second World War RAF bomber stations – among them Hemswell, Binbrook, Elsham Wolds and Scampton. During the war the skies echoed and the ground shook as squadron after squadron of bombers took off over the North Sea. Several of these bomber airfields are reputed to be haunted, perhaps because thousands of young men took off from there to meet terrible, untimely deaths. Often, as with RAF Hemswell, it is the control tower, the very heart of the station, where the ghostly manifestations take place. At Eltham Wolds, a dead pilot regularly appears in Second World War flying kit. At Scampton, once the home of 617 the Dambuster Squadron and now the home of the Dambuster Heritage Centre, the ghost of Wing Commander Guy Gibson VC himself has been seen in the nearby Petwood Hotel which used to be the Officers' Mess. He has appeared, smiling and relaxed, in the bar, that favourite place of all airmen, sometimes accompanied by his black Labrador, Nigger (a common name then for an all-black dog, but of course unacceptable now). The dog was adopted by 617 as its mascot but he always stayed close to his master – that is, until 16 May 1943 when, just before Gibson led 19 of the RAF's best crews to attack the Sorpe, Eder and Mohne dams, the dog inexplicably ran out into the road and was killed by a car. Before leaving, Gibson gave orders that his beloved pet should be buried at RAF Scampton between the perimeter fence and his office.

The dog's name was used as the code word to confirm the success of the raid, and it seems that the dog himself is still haunting the airfield. A black Labrador has frequently been seen running soundlessly about the airfield perimeter track, but disappears when approached. When the impressive Dambusters Memorial was opened in

nearby Woodhall Spa in May 1987, the choir from St Hilda's School sang at the official opening ceremony. As they posed in front of the memorial for a photograph, a black Labrador appeared and sat down in the middle of the group. He belonged to no one present, carried no identification and refused to leave until the photograph was taken. Then, as suddenly as he'd come, he disappeared.

Gainsborough Old Hall

LINCOLNSHIRE

This fine medieval manor house, one of the best preserved in the country, was built by Sir Thomas Burgh in around 1460. In the upstairs hall, the sad spectre of a broken-hearted woman has been seen, seemingly appearing out of a solid wall and then walking the length of the hall. It was only in the 1960s, during restoration work on the house, that a bricked-up doorway was discovered just where she materialised. The ghost is thought to be a daughter of one of the Burgh family who was refused permission to marry the man she loved. She also seems to have appeared to a child who lived opposite the hall, who said that a woman would often appear at an upstairs window and wave to him, but no-one else could ever see her.

Julian's Bower

LINCOLNSHIRE

The name is somewhat misleading because this is no leafy shelter but a series of winding paths cut into the ground to form a turf maze. Julian's Bower is one of the few surviving examples of these intriguing structures and is situated near the village of Alkborough on a strategic site where the Rivers Humber and Trent meet. Turf mazes were not designed to confuse like hedge mazes or labyrinths, but provide a clear, circuitous route round. They are believed to have a religious significance with the

centre representing Jerusalem and the way round a Crusade, or alternatively the journey through life struggling towards salvation. Mazes were obviously regarded as important religious symbols as they appear on the floors of several medieval cathedrals, and indeed the village church at Alkborough has replicas of Julian's Bower in the church porch and the chancel window.

The names given to some of the English mazes – Julian's Bower and The Walls of Troy, for instance – reflect the legend that mazes were brought to Italy by Julius, the son of Aeneas, the founder of Rome, after the Greeks had sacked the city of Troy. Roman origins have been claimed for Julian's Bower, while other theories maintain that it was cut in medieval times by the Benedictine monks from nearby Walcot. It is thought that they may have travelled along the maze paths on their knees for a penance, or as a substitute for embarking on a Crusade to the Holy Land.

By the Elizabethan period Julian's Bower resounded with childish laughter as the village youngsters used it to play games. At this time many turf mazes were obviously fast disappearing through lack of use: Shakespeare refers to mazes in *A Midsummer Night's Dream* that 'for lack of tread are indistinguishable'. However, children never seemed to have tired of treading Julian's Bower and it appears that their ghosts still do! The sound of young voices, laughter and singing have often been reported at the maze. One day in 1973, when an archaeologist brought his two young sons to visit the maze, the youngest soon became upset and tearful. After much coaxing, he finally explained that he wanted to play with the children in funny clothes who were skipping round the maze – but they wouldn't let him join in because he didn't know how to play their game. The parents couldn't help their tearful young son – because there were no other children there!

Thornton Abbey

Walking through the impressive 14th-century gateway, the visitor to the remains of this Augustinian friary gains a sense of the wealth and power this foundation once had. Yet all its riches could not buy peace, and a restless, malevolent spirit in the shape of a black monk is said to haunt the ruins, spelling death to anyone unfortunate enough to meet him. The ghost is believed to be Abbot Thomas de Gretham who deviated from his Christian faith to dabble in the occult and black arts.

The abbey was founded in 1139 as a house for Augustinian canons – priests who lived a communal life under the Rule of St Augustine and who also undertook various pastoral duties outside the abbey. It became rich and powerful, investing a great deal of money in an impressive building programme. Its wealth was a great attraction to Henry VIII who dissolved the abbey in 1539. In 1602 the abbey and its grounds were bought by Sir Vincent Skinner of Westminster. He demolished most of the buildings and began to erect a magnificent mansion. About this time, a skeleton was discovered in a small bricked-up chamber. Dressed in a black habit, and seated at a table on which there was a book, pen and inkwell, it was popularly believed to be the remains of the wicked Abbot Thomas.

It seems that the curse of this malevolent man affected the very stones of the abbey. Abraham de la Prynne, writing in 1697, relates that when Skinner 'built a most stately hall out of the same on the west side of the abbey plot within the moat, which hall when it was finished, fell quite down to the bare ground, without any visible cause'. The sudden collapse of the house was echoed in another venture. When Ferriby Sluice was built using stone from the old abbey, this project also failed.

OPPOSITE *The ghost of a former abbot, who dabbled in the black arts, has been seen in the gatehouse of Thornton Abbey.*

When the deed was done

    I heard among the solitary hills

Low breathings coming after me, and sounds

    Of undistinguishable motion, steps

Almost as silent as the turf they trod.

WILLIAM WORDSWORTH, 'THE PRELUDE'

Roche Abbey

SOUTH YORKSHIRE

Although smaller in size than other Cistercian abbeys like Rievaulx and Byland, Roche still boasts some of the finest early Gothic architecture in the country. Founded around 1180 in an isolated rocky valley, it survived until the Dissolution in the mid-16th century. As soon as the deed of surrender was signed on 23 June 1538, and before an orderly dismantling and auction could take place, a mob of local people descended on the abbey and, in a chaotic free-for-all, pillaged the stone, lead, tiles, paving, and anything else they thought might be useful.

The ruins that remained were neglected until they were in the ownership of the third Earl of Scarborough in the 18th century. This was the Romantic Age when desolation and solitude were regarded as the height of fashion – Mother Nature at her most sublime. As a result the abbey ruins were greatly admired. Horace Walpole, author of the Gothic novel *The Castle of Otranto*, wrote approvingly that they were 'hid in such a venerable chasm that you might lie concealed there even from a squire person of the parish. Lord Scarborough, to whom it belongs, neglects it as much as if he was afraid of ghosts.' Lord Scarborough was delighted that Roche was hailed as the epitome of romance, and commissioned Lancelot 'Capability' Brown to make the beautiful ruins even more picturesque. He was told to design a scheme that would appeal to the 'poet's feeling and painter's eye'. When the work was completed the abbey was adorned with grass parterres, terracing, waterfalls, numerous trees and an artificial lake with islands.

One thing remained constant – Roche's ghostly monks, who seem to have been silent witnesses to the many changes. There are the inevitable numerous tales of monkish figures, one of the most frequently reported being a man dressed in a long white habit (like the ones worn by Cistercian monks) who walks the ruins with a pronounced limp. In 1987 he appeared to two children near the old monks' cemetery near the church, terrifying them with his ghostly pallor and gaunt, skull-like face. A few years later, an Austrian tourist, whose 'painter's eye' had been captivated by the ruins, was sketching on a hot summer's afternoon when he got that uncomfortable feeling of 'eyes boring into the back of the head'. He looked round quickly and clearly saw the ghostly monk standing just behind him – before it turned away and slowly disappeared through an ancient wall.

Conisbrough Castle

SOUTH YORKSHIRE

Sir Walter Scott's first sighting of the spectacular white cylindrical keep of this 12th-century castle provided some of the inspiration for his novel *Ivanhoe*. Built of magnesian limestone, it is the only one of its kind in England and is a classic of medieval architecture. However, Scott never saw one of the castle's many ghosts. They include the ubiquitous grey monk, and an unhappy grey lady who is seen at the top of the keep where she reputedly met her death. Then there are strange shimmering lights that seem to come from the area where the chapel once stood and perhaps are the ghostly gleam from long-extinguished candles. Strange noises have been heard too – hushed voices whispering in corners and the sound of something heavy bumping down the stairs.

Brodsworth Hall

SOUTH YORKSHIRE

This fine Victorian mansion, set in beautiful country just south of Doncaster, was the home of the Thellusson family until 1990 when the daughter of the last family member to live there gave it to the nation. It was built in the 1860s by Charles Sabine Thellusson, who was one of the two final beneficiaries of the strange and famous will made by his ancestor, Peter Thellusson, who had died in 1797. This will – said to be the inspiration for the *Jarndyce v Jarndyce* case in Charles Dickens' *Bleak House* – left various bequests to immediate family but directed that the remainder of the massive estate should be left to accumulate during the lifetime of all the sons, grandsons and great-grandsons who were alive at Peter Thellusson's death. Only on the death of the last of these family members, in 1856, could the estate be distributed.

Brodsworth has many ghost stories, the strangest and most recent of which is perhaps that told by Mary, nurse towards the end of her life of Sylvia Grant-Dalton who was the last of the family to live there. Charles Sabine Thellusson had had a large family, including several sons, but the only one to produce children was his youngest daughter, Constance, who had married Horace Grant-Dalton in 1883. Sylvia was the wife of Constance's son Charles Grant-Dalton, and lived at Brodsworth all her life until her death in 1988. Her nurse Mary relates that every night, on her way up to bed, Sylvia would put her head round the door of the room known as the Lathe Room and say 'Goodnight, Charles.' By this time the room had become a depository for all sorts of family rubbish, including a rocking chair (which has since disappeared). Mary herself on several occasions witnessed the chair rocking although no-one was seated in it. She has told staff at the house that she was never sure which Charles Sylvia was addressing – possibly her husband, but perhaps an earlier member of the family, even Charles Sabine himself.

Mary saw several other ghostly manifestations at Brodsworth, including doorknobs on the door of the Mistress's Bedroom turning by themselves late at night – incidents always accompanied by manic barking and

OPPOSITE *Victorian Brodsworth Hall which is alive with paranormal phenomena.*

rushing around by the family dogs. The Master's Bedroom next door has seen appearances of a man in Edwardian dress sitting in a chair, thought to be the ghost of Augustus Thellusson who died in 1931. And there are several others: a woman in a long Victorian dress on the library stairs; a man in khaki uniform on the same stairs; two female figures, possibly Sylvia Grant-Dalton and her last long-term housekeeper, Emily Chester, standing at the foot of the main stairs in the entrance hall, smiling and watching visitors walk past; even a ginger cat on the bedroom corridor…

Staff at Brodsworth have their own stories to tell. There are many parts of the building where they experience cold spots and the feeling of being watched, and several of them have felt that something was pushing past them in the basement, near the room that is now used as the staff room, and have glimpsed something out of the corner of their eyes. One staff member has experienced an even odder sensation on several occasions: while doing a guided tour of parts of the house not normally open to visitors, she has tried to enter Bedroom 8 in the servants' wing and felt something physically pushing her back. She is unable to enter the room, but other people within the group can.

The witches of Pendle

In the late 16th and early 17th centuries the forces of evil were widely feared, and there were strong superstitions about how women, in particular, could be lured into becoming agents of the devil. Wise women and 'white' witches were well known and accepted in their communities, but it was thought that it was all too easy to be seduced into following the black arts instead. In 1597 King James VI of Scotland had published his famous treatise *Daemonologie*, later Anglicised and reprinted when he also became King of England as James I; and in 1606 William Shakespeare had great success with his new drama featuring three witches that we still superstitiously refer to as 'the Scottish play'.

Pendle Hill, the vast flat-topped hill that has been nicknamed the 'roof of Lancashire', is notoriously associated with witchcraft. In August 1612 three generations of so-called witches were hanged at Lancaster after what was described as 'The wonderful discovery of witches in Lancashire'. Known as the Pendle witches because they lived near Pendle Hill, the majority of them were simple, uneducated folk who were so terrified by the authorities that they would admit anything and implicate anyone against whom they had a grudge. One of them was an elderly woman known as Old Demdike, who lived at Malkin Tower and was accused of holding covens, practising black arts and plotting to blow up Lancaster Castle. She admitted the charges, and more and more women were implicated as fear and rumours spread. Finally, 19 women were accused of witchcraft. They all admitted guilt except Alice Nutter of Roughlee Hall. Alice came from a different background from the others and was a staunch Catholic. However, she was identified as being at a coven at Malkin Tower and went to the scaffold still protesting her innocence. Only Old Demdike escaped the hangman's noose as she died in prison before sentence could be carried out.

In 1633 another large group of witches was identified in the area. Edmund Robinson, a young boy, claimed that he found a pair of greyhounds loose on the moors one day. Suddenly they turned into two witches. He instantly recognised them as being two local women and reported them. Amazingly, his story was believed and he was even sent on missions to identify other witches in the local community. After numerous women had been accused and hanged, he confessed he'd made the whole thing up. Today this alarming period in Lancashire's history is commemorated at the Pendle Heritage Centre.

Whalley Abbey Gatehouse

LANCASHIRE

The late 13th-century gatehouse of this important Cistercian abbey, founded in 1296, now spans a narrow lane, but this was once the main route northwards up the Ribble Valley. This explains the imposing architecture of the main entrance to the monastic precinct of what was to become the second richest monastery in Lancashire. In the early 16th century its last abbot, John Paslew, 'not only lived like a lord, but also travelled like one', according to the contemporary historian Owen Ashmore. In 1520, however, Paslew was visited by the ghost of a former monk of Whalley called Edmund Howard, who foretold that Paslew would live for another 16 years and no more. Sure enough, 16 years later, Paslew became implicated in the Pilgrimage of Grace, the northern rebellion against Henry VIII. He lit the beacon on Pendle Hill as the signal to start the Pilgrimage and refused to take the oath of allegiance to the king. He was tried in Lancaster, found guilty of high treason and executed on 9 March 1537 at Lancaster. However, local tradition has always maintained that he was hanged at the abbey gates and buried in Whalley churchyard. The ghost of the abbot has been seen many times around Whalley and has even been caught on film! There is now a conference and training centre on the site of the abbey, but it seems that the monks are still there as well. Astonished witnesses have seen ghostly processions of monks, and have heard chanting, measured footsteps along passageways and doors closing in empty rooms; some have even had the feeling of someone sitting down on the edge of a bed.

Spofforth Castle

NORTH YORKSHIRE

In October 1969 a party of schoolchildren and their teacher were studying this ancient fortified manor house, once owned by the powerful Percy family, when they witnessed a terrifying sight. They saw the top half of a woman at the top of the 13th-century tower, and then suddenly, before their horrified gaze, she seemed to leap from the tower even though she was still only visible from the waist up. But before her body could hit the ground, she simply vanished. This was just another of the many reported sightings of the mysterious suicidal lady who always seems to be surrounded by a blueish light.

The city of a thousand ghosts

York is renowned for its fascinating and spooky ghost stories. One of them is a huge black dog with blood-red eyes who stalks the 'snickleways' – the narrow, winding medieval streets. Known as 'a barguist' in this part of the country, it is a portent of doom. These phantom black dogs are reported all over England, inspiring terror and imagination. Who can forget Sir Arthur Conan Doyle's *The Hound of the Baskervilles*?

In St Mary's Abbey a shade known as the Black Monk lurks among the ruins, and in the 18th-century Theatre Royal there is a grey nun, as well as the ghost of an actor who was accidentally killed during a stage fight. Dean Gale still sits in his pew in the Minster keeping a watch over the place he worked so hard for, and where he was buried in 1702. Many of the city's pubs are the haunt of phantoms ranging from spectral cats to the ghost of playboy George Villiers, Duke of Buckingham, who has a particular fancy for haunting women, especially when they're naked!

One of the most famous apparitions was reported in 1953 at the Treasurer's House in the Minster Yard. A young plumber called Harry Martindale was working down in the cellar when he heard the sound of a horn. Looking up, he was stunned to see a man on horseback appear out of the wall. The man was dressed in Roman uniform and was soon followed by a whole cohort of ghostly Roman soldiers who marched dejectedly across the cellar and disappeared into the opposite wall. But, stranger still, they didn't seem to have any feet and were only visible from the knees upwards! The reason was not hard to find. Buried below the floor of the cellar an old Roman road was discovered.

Clifford's Tower

YORK

This stone tower atop its grassy mound – originally part of York Castle, and first built in wood by William I a couple of years after his conquest of England – is the site of one of the region's most famous and eerie supernatural phenomena. At certain times the solid stone walls appear to drip with blood.

In 1190 there were riots in York as anti-Semitic fervour gripped the city. Grumblings about the large Jewish community had quickly grown to violence as some of the city's inhabitants, led by Richard Malebisse and an unknown friar, vowed to purge York of all Jews. As the mob gathered strength, many Jews fled their homes and sought refuge in the tower where they barricaded themselves in. However, the rioters stormed the tower which was set alight. As the flames licked round them, most of the Jews determined on death rather than surrender and committed mass suicide. The rest were massacred by the mob when they finally stormed the tower.

Completely destroyed in the fire, the tower had to be rebuilt – this time in stone quarried from nearby Tadcaster. But, soon after its construction, a red fluid seemed to be oozing from the walls. The appalling end to the anti-Jewish riot had left the city with an overwhelming feeling of horror and disgust, and so it was natural for the inhabitants to think that this was the vengeance of the Jews. Their blood dripping down the walls of the place where they had met their death was a constant reminder to the city of its persecution. Scientific tests have now shown that the red stains are caused by iron oxide in the stone. But there is a twist to the tale: none of the other stone taken from that quarry has ever contained iron oxide.

In addition to those who have reported seeing the 'blood', others claim to have actually been there in a previous life. Under hypnosis, several people have given detailed descriptions of their experiences. One woman reverted to being a young Jewess called 'Rebecca' living in York in 1190 and gave a graphic account of medieval life in the city. 'Rebecca' described how she and her family had managed to escape from Clifford's Tower and hide from the mob in the crypt of St Mary's Church in Castlegate. However, the rioters tracked them down and 'Rebecca' and all her family were murdered. A fantastic story – particularly because St Mary's has no crypt. But then, in 1975, workmen discovered a burial chamber below the floor of the church that exactly matched 'Rebecca's' description of the Jewish family's hiding place.

The bloody history of the tower continued into the 14th century when its then owner, Roger de Clifford, took part in a rebellion against Edward II. Defeated at the Battle of Boroughbridge in 1322, Clifford was executed and his body was dangled in chains from the battlements of the tower. From that time on it has been known as Clifford's Tower.

Skipsea Castle
EAST YORKSHIRE

A ruthless Norman lord built this motte-and-bailey castle in the 12th century. Drogo de Bevere, first Earl of Holderness, married the niece of William of Conqueror, so securing favour at court. But the marriage was purely one of convenience and Drogo soon became disenchanted with his bride. So he prepared a love potion laced with deadly poison, and his poor wife trustingly drank it. As soon as she was dead, Drogo sprang onto the fleetest horse in his stable and galloped as fast as he could to William's court. Cold-bloodedly bluffing his way, Drogo succeeded in borrowing a great deal of money and then he was off again – this time to the nearest port. He escaped to the Continent before the fate of his wife was discovered. From then on the ghostly white figure of Lady de Bevere has been seen around the castle, and even after hundreds of years her wronged spirit has still not been laid to rest.

There is also a legend that two brothers, on different sides in one of the county's civil wars, fought a duel on the castle ramparts. Apparently four deep footprints can still be seen and no grass will grow over the spot where they battled.

Scarborough Castle
NORTH YORKSHIRE

There can be few better defensive locations than Scarborough Castle's. It is situated on a grassy headland surrounded by precipitous cliffs and is only connected to the mainland by a narrow strip of land. The strategic importance of the promontory has been recognised for thousands of years, and late Bronze Age and early Iron Age settlements have been discovered on the site. The headland was later used as a lookout station by the Romans and, in the 10th century, Viking raiders took a liking to the sheltered harbour below the cliff and decided to stay. They named their settlement or burh after their leader Thorgil who was nicknamed Skarthi (Harelip).

There was certainly a castle at Scarborough by the early 12th century, and it was taken over and developed by Henry II who recognised how useful the site could be as a royal power base. Even today, in its ruined state, it is obvious what an incredibly impressive place it once was.

But don't visit it alone! A headless ghost reputedly appears to solitary visitors and tries to drive them over the battlements to plunge to their deaths on the rocks below. It is said to be the vengeful spirit of Piers Gaveston who was governor of Scarborough Castle in the early 14th century. Gaveston was the favourite of Edward II, but he had made enemies of the barons who resented his influence over the king. They decided to dispose of him and besieged the castle in 1312. Gaveston held out as long as he could but finally surrendered after being promised a safe passage to London for trial. But this promise was broken by Gaveston's arch enemy, the Earl of Warwick, who seized Gaveston on the journey south and promptly beheaded him.

Two other ghosts are also reputed to haunt the castle site. Richard III has been seen on the battlements looking out to sea and watching for his fleet, and a Roman soldier appears on the cliff top near the Roman signal station.

ABOVE *Overlooking the bleak North Sea, Scarborough Castle has a violent past.*

Whitby Abbey

The stark outline of the abbey ruins high on the headland are eerie enough in themselves – especially when a blood-red sunset seeps through the window tracery. It is rather odd that Whitby has attracted such a reputation for horror because it is a very important religious site and the cradle of northern Christianity. But there are also a whole host of ghosts associated with this amazing place, especially St Hilda, who founded the abbey in AD 680 and appears at one of the windows dressed in a white shroud. This apparition intrigued Bram Stoker, who included it in his classic horror story *Dracula* by making his heroine Mina refer to the ghostly figure in her diary. Dracula himself, of course, first landed at Whitby in the guise of a great black dog.

Then there is the weeping ghost of Constance de Beverley, a nun who lost her heart to a knight called Marmion. She was locked in a dungeon for her sin and appears, pleading for release, on the steps leading down to her prison. This story was adapted by Sir Walter Scott in 'Marmion'.

At dawn on the old Christmas Day (about 6 January) a phantom choir sings in the ruins, and a coach pulled by headless horses has been seen going through the abbey and then plunging over the nearby clifftop.

Apart from the horror stories there is also a charming legend associated with Whitby. A young boy lived there, looking after the animals owned by the nuns and sleeping in one of the barns alongside his charges. One day he was startled when a bright light suddenly enveloped him and he heard a voice telling him to make songs of praise. The boy finally plucked up the courage to tell the nuns about his strange experience and ask them what it meant. They wisely told him that it had been a vision of his future and he must follow his calling. This he did, becoming Caedman – the father of English song.

OPPOSITE *The eerie clifftop silhouette of Whitby Abbey.*

Pickering Castle

NORTH YORKSHIRE

William the Conqueror built the first castle on this strategically important site, and it remained in the hands of the royal family for many centuries. Around 1326 a tower was built to protect the west postern gate, and it became known as Rosamund's Tower, seemingly reflecting a tragedy that had happened more than a century before. Henry II, king of England and owner of Pickering Castle in the early 13th century, had fallen in love with a great beauty, Rosamund Clifford, known as 'Fair Rosamund'. Henry was, however, already married to Eleanor of Aquitaine and so Rosamund became his mistress. Eleanor was none too happy with this arrangement, especially when Rosamund had Henry's child, and so she ruthlessly ended the relationship by forcing Rosamund to drink poison and so suffer a dreadful death. Her legend, however, lived on and local people ensured that Fair Rosamund would always be associated with the royal castle by giving the tower her name.

You would expect that Fair Rosamund would be the one to haunt the castle, but in fact the resident ghost is yet another grey monk. He was seen in the 1950s by a custodian who described the apparition as a tall monk wearing a long, grey, hooded robe walking across the castle grounds towards the keep. Unlike other ghostly monks, this one seems to be carrying something as his arms are stretched out in front of him. There was a chapel in the castle grounds as early as the 13th century, and records reveal that there was a resident chaplain at the castle, supported by a royal income, until 1547 when Henry VIII suppressed such posts.

Helmsley Castle

YORKSHIRE

Set in a stunning landscape in Ryedale on the edge of the North York Moors, Helmsley has been an important settlement since Saxon times. This ancient market town is dominated by the impressive remains of the castle established in the 1120s by the powerful baron, Walter Espec, as the residence at the 'head of his honour' in the centre of his Yorkshire estates. One of Henry I's 'new men' and an enthusiastic supporter of religious reform, he was an important influence in this part of the country, founding the first northern Cistercian abbey in England at Rievaulx and an Augustinian priory at Kirkham. Subsequent owners made their own alterations to the castle and in the 16th century a fine Tudor mansion was built inside the massive earthworks. The castle was besieged for three months in 1644 during the Civil War when the castle was garrisoned by Royalist troops. They finally had to surrender due to lack of food and the Parliamentarians blew up parts of the castle to prevent it being used again. Perhaps the ghost of a soldier seen sitting forlornly on the ruins is the spectre of a vanquished Cavalier.

The castle came into the ownership of the notorious rake George Villiers, Duke of Buckingham, in the 17th century and he spent his last years here until he caught his death of a chill in 1685 while out hunting. He is immortalised in the nursery rhyme 'Georgie Porgie Pudding and Pie, kissed the girls and made them cry.' The ghost of a green lady who appears both inside and outside the castle is thought to date from this period of the castle's history. She has been seen many times, her soft green dress rustling as she passes people walking their dogs late at night near the castle, but there are no clues to her identity – nor to whether she was one of the girls Georgie Porgie made to cry.

Weird pixie-like creatures are reported to roam near the castle and the surrounding countryside. The town itself also has its fair share of spectres. A white lady reputedly walks the courtyard behind the church and the Black Swan, one of Helmsley's famous coaching inns, has a phantom baby. On several occasions guests at the inn have complained that they were kept awake all night by a crying infant, only to find that no babies were staying there. The heart-rending wails are reputed to come from a ghostly baby walled up there centuries ago by its unmarried mother, distraught at the disgrace of having an illegitimate child.

OPPOSITE *The gaunt ruins of Helmsley Castle loom over the town.*

Rievaulx Abbey

NORTH YORKSHIRE

Eight hundred years ago St Aelred, one of the early abbots of this wonderful Cistercian abbey, described it as: 'Everywhere peace, everywhere serenity, and a marvellous freedom from the tumult of the world.' The monks must have loved this beautiful place and their everyday life still seems to be imprinted on the atmosphere. Many people have heard the pealing of bells coming from the ruins and recently one visitor staying overnight in a nearby guesthouse complained that he hadn't been able to get a wink of sleep because of the regular tolling of a church bell. No peace and serenity for him!

Byland Abbey

NORTH YORKSHIRE

In the 12th century this abbey was described as one of the three shining lights of northern monasticism, along with Fountains and Byland's neighbour, Rievaulx. It had the largest Cistercian church in Britain at that time, and even today it is easy to imagine how it would have looked in its former glory with shafts of light radiating through the great rose window in the west end speckling the bowed heads of the monastic congregation with myriad colours. It was a flourishing community, and daily life went on in the simple ordered way of Cistercian rule – until one day in the 13th century when a UFO arrived! *The Chronicle of William of Newburgh* in 1290 reports that the abbot was about to say grace when one of the monks burst in to announce that there was 'a great portent' outside. Everyone rushed outside and saw a large silver disc hovering in the sky above them which 'excited the greatest terror'. Another contemporary manuscript, *Historica Anglorum* by Matthew Paris, records a similar event.

In about 1400, one of the monks of the abbey wrote twelve ghost stories on the blank pages of a much older manuscript. They reflected the Catholic faith of the writer, being mainly concerned with tortured spirits who needed absolution for sins they had committed while they were still alive. Many of the stories describe the ghosts as taking on the forms of animals and birds such as horses, dogs or, in one case, a crow spurting streams of fire. These

imaginative tales, which no doubt thrilled the monks at Byland, were published by that great ghost story writer, M R James.

With all the years spent constructing the abbey's splendid buildings and the strong spiritual force that bound the community together, it is not surprising that 12th-century life still seems to carry on in another time zone to ours. Sometimes the two zones seem to overlap. One recent occasion was in 1996, on the late May bank holiday, when the abbey was holding a special event to attract visitors. Entitled 'A Day in the Life of an Abbey', it was a chance for children and their parents to find out what religious life actually entailed, with a Latin Mass, a chapter house meeting and a silent meal in the refectory all being re-enacted by a specialist group. The final attraction was a 'beating of the bounds' ceremony with shouts of 'Out! Out! Out!' at every exit to oust the Devil. Halfway through this, the heavens opened and a torrential downpour put an end to the proceedings. The rain continued unabated for four hours, so saturating the ground that the re-enactment group could not put up their tents for the night. Some elected to sleep in their cars, but others were given permission to spend the night in the site museum which had the advantage of being dry but the disadvantage that there was no electricity. Everyone settled down as best they could on the hard stone floor and Bill, one of the group, found a spot next to a plinth supporting two grave covers. He curled up in his sleeping bag with his back against the stone plinth and went to sleep. All was quiet until the early hours of the morning when Bill was suddenly woken by someone gently, but insistently, rocking his hip. It felt as though someone behind him was trying to shake him awake, but when he looked round he realised that that was impossible – only the stone plinth was behind him! The time he had been woken was around 2 am when the monks would have woken each other to go down to the church for Matins, the first service of the day.

OPPOSITE The imposing remains of Byland Abbey, the scene of a 13th-century UFO sighting.

Middleham Castle

NORTH YORKSHIRE

Known as the 'Windsor of the North', this castle was built in the 12th century on the site of an earlier Norman fortification. It was the favourite castle of Richard III who grew up here. This is one of the many places where there is a legendary hidden treasure. All you have to do to find it is to run three times round the castle and then, where you stop, that's where the treasure is hidden. Sounds too good to be true, doesn't it? And it is. After all, where would you start?

Ghostly crews of RAF Leeming

Not far from Middleham, on the other side of the Great North Road, RAF Leeming has the reputation of being one of the most haunted airfields in Britain. It was opened as a bomber airfield during the desperate effort to rearm in 1940, and in 1943 became No 63 Royal Canadian Air Force base. The squadron flew Halifax bombers, heavy aircraft that struggled up night after night over the Yorkshire countryside. Like so many RAF stations, Leeming suffered heavy casualties as badly damaged aircraft strove to reach home, some reaching base only to crash on landing. Not surprisingly, one of Leeming's manifestations is a sudden fiery glow in the centre of the runway from which ghostly figures emerge and then disappear. The glow comes from the spot where a Halifax bomber crashed and burst into flames, killing all the crew.

Another Leeming ghost is a pilot in a Second World War Mae West and flying helmet. He appears in one of the servicing hangars, calling for his crew. According to legend, the pilot was accidentally crushed to death there while inspecting his Halifax after repairs. This hangar is not the only one to be haunted. Another is known for its eerie atmosphere, and workmen and cleaners have reported strange sounds, sudden drops in temperature and ghostly voices. One night, people standing outside the apparently locked and empty hangar saw all the lights come on and then heard the sound of voices inside. The security officers were called but a thorough search revealed nothing. To ensure airfield safety, they locked two of their trained Alsatian guard dogs in the hangar overnight. In the morning, the dogs were so distressed and unmanageable that they had to be destroyed.

Richmond Castle

NORTH YORKSHIRE

There are a number of myths associated with Richmond and its magnificent castle, built by the Normans on high ground overlooking the River Swale. One claims that the first bridge over the river that led to the founding of the original town was actually a thank-you present from the Devil. He was apparently extremely grateful to a poor shepherd who had taken him home one day and fed him after he had got lost and disorientated in the Yorkshire Dales. In the castle itself, the Gold Hole Tower is deemed to have earned its name because there is a treasure trove buried somewhere inside it.

The two most famous folk tales associated with the site both have their counterparts in other places. The first is similar to one associated with Housesteads, on Hadrian's Wall in Northumberland – that King Arthur and the knights of the Round Table slumber in a cave below the castle waiting to be summoned to England's aid. It is claimed that Arthur's last battle was either at Catterick or on the slopes of the Eston Hills, and there are many hopeful legends that he and his knights are not dead but merely sleeping somewhere.

In Richmond, so the story goes, there once lived a man named Potter Thompson who was married to a harridan of a wife. One day, in order to escape her constant carping, he took a long walk and eventually ended up below the castle. Pausing for a rest, his eye was suddenly caught by a gap in the rocky escarpment which appeared to be the entrance to a cave. Intrigued, he looked in and saw a long passage with a faint light glowing at one end. Potter Thompson, following the light, found himself in a vast cavern and there, fast asleep, were a king and knights dressed in full armour. He instantly recognised King Arthur because there, displayed on a table in the centre of the cavern, were a horn and the famous sword,

OPPOSITE *King Arthur and the knights of the Round Table are said to sleep in a cave beneath Richmond Castle.*

Excalibur. Excited that he had been lucky enough to discover the resting place of King Arthur, Potter Thompson decided to take Excalibur in order to prove that his story was true. But, as he started to pull the sword from its scabbard, the sleeping knights started to stir. The terrified Thompson took to his heels, but not before a sorrowful voice had intoned this verse:

> *Potter Thompson, Potter Thompson,*
> *If thou hadst either drawn*
> *The sword, or blown the horn,*
> *Thou wouldst have been the luckiest man*
> *That ever yet was born.*

As soon as he found himself outside again in the sunshine, Thompson began to feel a little better and a little braver. He realised that, if he went back for the sword or the horn, all his troubles would be over. So, taking a deep breath, he turned back to the entrance of the cave. But it had gone. Frantically, he searched all over the rocky banks of the castle but never again was the secret tunnel revealed to him.

The story of Arthur and his knights, along with another persistent rumour that there is a secret tunnel linking the castle with nearby Easby Abbey, intrigued a regiment of soldiers who were stationed in Richmond many years after Potter Thompson had lived in the town. They decided to stage a methodical search of all the cells and dungeons to see if they could find the entrance to a secret passage. There was great excitement when one of the soldiers discovered a small aperture which seemed,

when a light was put into it, to extend down into a long tunnel. The excitement was short-lived, however, when they realised that no-one was small enough to squeeze into the hole. Then someone had the bright idea that their young drummer boy might just fit. The lad was only about ten years old and none too keen on the idea of being pushed into a dark hole, but his fellow soldiers bribed him to agree. They assured him that all would be well and that he was to beat his drum as he went so that they could track his progress. The gallant boy squeezed through the hole and wriggled away, pausing every now and then to bang the drum. The sound carried on and on and on – but the boy never returned. No other person was small enough to go and find him, and it is said that he is still down there doomed to beat his drum for eternity. Sometimes the sound of drumbeats are heard near the river, and at other times they seem to come up from the ground near the medieval ruins of Easby Abbey as the poor Drummer Boy of Richmond Castle continues his quest.

Pendragon Castle

CUMBRIA

Arthurian legends abound in Cumbria and this castle, set in the beautiful Mallerstang gorge near Kirkby Stephen, is said to be built on the site of a 5th-century fortress constructed by Uther Pendragon, King Arthur's father. He reputedly settled here after killing a dragon-serpent that was terrorising the region, and he is also meant to have tried unsuccessfully to divert the River Eden to make a moat round his home. In old age he took up arms once again against the Angles, and died here after drinking from a water supply poisoned by his enemies.

The ruins date to the 12th century when, in 1173, another castle was built by Hugh de Morville. It later passed into the hands of the powerful Clifford family who also owned Appleby and Brough castles. With Arthurian links and stories of Merlin living here and visiting Castlerigg Stone Circle, it is not surprising that many sightings of supernatural phenomena have been reported. White ladies glide round the castle at night and, when moonbeams cloak the ruins in an eerie glow, a ghostly horseman is seen galloping soundlessly towards the castle. Whether he is the mortally sick Uther Pendragon returning home after battle, a frantic messenger or a warrior of the mighty Clifford clan, no one will ever know.

Perhaps the most bizarre ghost story in the country is associated with this site. A rich treasure is meant to lie buried in the castle's foundations, but anyone rash enough to try and dig for the gold will be confronted by a vast, spectral, black – hen! This ghostly chicken scratches and pecks at all the earth excavated by the hapless treasure-seeker, and ensures that the hole is filled in again!

Castlerigg Stone Circle

CUMBRIA

Stone circles are weird in themselves. Why would anyone drag enormous lumps of stone across the most inaccessible terrain and then laboriously set them into the ground?

However, although we can't be certain what they were originally intended for, these monuments, predating the pyramids and constructed in an age when only crude stone tools were available to their builders, are simply awesome. Castlerigg is one of the most numinous, standing high up in the Lake District overlooking the Thirlmere Valley with the mountains of High Seat and Helvellyn forming a dramatic backdrop. Strangely, the assorted shapes of the standing stones seem to echo the form of the surrounding hills. Was this the intention of its original builders or just a fluke?

Built around 3000 BC, Castlerigg is one of the earliest stone circles in the country. It was originally made up of 42 stones, but now there are 38 in an open circle, with an unusual rectangular cove of standing stones in the centre. Try counting them and see if you come up with the same number. The stones are strangely difficult to count and even experts seem to differ.

There is definitely a strange atmosphere here, helped no doubt by its wild landscape setting. There have been many reports of eerie blue lights which seem to flit between the stones. Maybe this unusual iridescence is caused by a geological fault that allows gases to escape the earth's crust... or perhaps Neolithic people saw these same blue lights and decided to set their stones here in what appeared to be a magical place. Or again, they might be the phantom lights from some ancient pagan ritual. Whatever their cause, it is interesting to note that the phenomena of moving blue lights are reported from many other stone circle sites around the country.

Penrith Castle

CUMBRIA

The castle was constructed around 1397 as another bastion of protection against the marauding Scots who had burnt down the town of Penrith in 1345. It later became a royal castle, before being badly damaged in the Civil War when it was the headquarters of General Lambert and his Parliamentarian army. Although the castle had been dismantled in the 1650s and there were no soldiers in the area, a farm labourer was startled on Midsummer's Eve in 1735 to see an army marching across the fell not far from the castle. Everyone to whom he told his story thought he'd been out in the sun too long or supped too much ale. However, a couple of years later, again on Midsummer's Eve, several people witnessed the phantom army marching five abreast across the fell. It seems that over the next few years more and more people saw this strange sight, and each time the army seemed to have grown in size. Eventually it included cavalry and carriages as well as foot soldiers, and the silent procession took quite a time to pass over the hilltop. That it was a spiritual force rather than a real one was confirmed when no hoofprint, footstep or carriage wheel mark could be seen the next day.

Lanercost Priory

CUMBRIA

The ruins of a 12th-century priory, set in the turbulent borderland between Scotland and England and against the dramatic backdrop of the Cumbrian fells, are the perfect spot for a spectre. This Augustinian priory has been a centre of Christian worship for centuries and Lanercost still seems to echo with chants and whispered devotion. Its position always meant that it was vulnerable to attack, and in the 14th century it was raided by the legendary Robert the Bruce himself. So, is the phantom which stalks the area of the great transept crossing arches the ghost of a monk, a Scots soldier – or a tomcat? It is in fact one of the most unusual ghosts in English Heritage properties – a ginger cat. Ghosts come in all shapes and sizes but their colour is fairly uniform – shades of grey and pale blue are usually preferred. Bright orange ghosts are incredibly rare.

However, there have been numerous sightings of the cat, which likes to rest on a table-top tomb when it is not walking through the transept. When approached it disappears into thin air. An Australian visitor who knew nothing about the ginger cat wrote to Lanercost to report seeing a 'soft orange light' under the great crossing arch and asking what it could possibly be. She said that the glow had brought with it an enveloping sense of peace which had been with her ever since. Perhaps it is a trick of the light, or a real cat with a fondness for ruins. However, it is interesting that the great crossing arches under the tower were the most difficult part of the building to construct, and medieval builders had ways of ensuring success which had nothing to do with Christianity: the pagan ritual sacrifice of a cat would have done the trick.

The ghost of a wronged woman is said to haunt Naworth stream which wends its way past the priory to Naworth Castle, once the home of the Dacre family. She threw herself into the water and drowned after learning that Lord Dacre, who was her lover and the father of her illegitimate son, had married another. Legend has it that Lord Dacre and his bride discovered the body in the river and were cursed by the grieving mother of the dead girl with the words:

Oh, cursed the cruel hand that wrought this hour to me,
May evil grim aye follow him until the day he dee.

The distraught mother's words seemed to have little effect on the health and happiness of the newlyweds and they were soon blessed with a son. But a couple of years later the little boy fell off his rocking horse and died. There were no more children and so the line of the Dacres of Naworth came to an end.

OPPOSITE *Lanercost Priory, where a phantom ginger cat walks the area near the great crossing arch.*
OVERLEAF *The ruins of Lanercost Priory, which resonate with echoes of the past.*

The end of Lanercost Priory came in the early 16th century with the Dissolution of the Monasteries. This fate had apparently been foretold by a witch who had prophesied:

> When a bull shall toll the Lanercost bell,
> And a hare bring forth on Naworth's hearth stone,
> Lanercost shall fall, Naworth be burnt down
> And Dalstone church be washed away.

The prophesy has nearly come true. Lanercost is now in ruins and much of Naworth was destroyed by fire in 1844. Only Dalstone church has so far escaped its doom – but, as it is situated on the Solway plain, global warming may yet see the Firth lapping ever closer.

Carlisle Castle

CUMBRIA

There is an intriguing mystery associated with this Norman castle. The skeleton of a woman was discovered bricked up in one of the walls when alterations were being made in the 19th century. She was dressed in tartan and wearing expensive rings and jewellery, but there seems to have been no clue to her identity.

In 1842 a sentry was patrolling when he was suddenly confronted by a mysterious grey figure. It didn't move or speak when challenged and so the sentry lunged at it with his bayonet. The blade met no resistance, passing through the figure which slowly disappeared in front of his eyes. The sentry was discovered in a state of profound shock, but managed to tell his amazing story to his fellow soldiers before collapsing and dying a few hours later.

Were the two incidents related? Was the ghost seen by the sentry the spirit of the Scots lady? Or could it have been one of the other tormented souls who suffered and died here? After all, the castle has witnessed many a bloody battle with the Scots as it strove to protect England's border. It was also the prison for a while of Mary, Queen of Scots, who was incarcerated in a number of places around the country and whose restless spirit has been well documented. Later, supporters of Bonnie Prince Charlie were imprisoned and executed here after their attempt to hold the castle was quelled by the Hanoverian army. The famous 'licking stones' in the castle cells have reputedly been worn smooth by the tongues of the poor prisoners licking the walls to get enough moisture to stay alive.

Spoof spectre of Carlisle

The city of Carlisle was terrified by a 'ghost' in 1872. The appearance of the apparition was reported by the local paper, the *Carlisle Herald*, which described how a tall white figure had been seen in various parts of the city, only to mysteriously disappear. This was a most persistent ghost – it began popping up everywhere and eventually people were too scared to go out after dark. Before long it was appearing in the daytime as well and soon near hysteria was gripping Carlisle, with women refusing to venture even to church on a Sunday unless accompanied by 'the sterner sex'. However, the newspaper was sceptical and firmly believed the ghost to be the work of a prankster. But despite the reassurances of the paper, people were still too scared to challenge the ghost when it appeared. Finally, a group of brave youths decided that enough was enough. Arming themselves with pitchforks, they lay in wait by one of the ghost's favourite routes through the city. Sure enough, the ghostly white figure appeared. The gang stepped out to confront it, but completely lost their bottle when the ghost hurtled towards them in a most menacing fashion. They turned tail and ran as fast as their legs could carry them. The newspaper published another article warning the so-called ghost that unless these hauntings ceased, the culprit risked being injured or killed – because next time the citizens of Carlisle might arm themselves with guns. The ghost took the advice and completely vanished.

Hadrian's Wall (Housesteads)

NORTHUMBERLAND

The 73-mile wall constructed by the Romans at the beginning of the 2nd century AD to keep out the Scots and Picts is now a World Heritage Site and snakes across the country from Wallsend in the east to Maryport in the west. The blood of countless battles has soaked into the soil and this is a place where patriotic fervour and strong emotions resonate. Considering its long, tormented history it is hardly surprising that a few Romans still stalk the wall.

Rather surprisingly, however, most of the stories on Hadrian's Wall are associated with that most English of kings, Arthur, who seems to crop up in all parts of the British Isles. Housesteads is the best preserved fort on the Wall and, just a couple of miles east of it, the wall winds its way over a rocky outcrop called Sewingshields Crag, once the site of a small castle. Local legend tells of a

shepherd who was sitting in the ruins of the castle, knitting as he watched over his flock. The ball of wool slipped from his fingers and tumbled down the crag, unwinding as it went. Anxious not to lose the wool he had taken so long to spin, the shepherd followed the length of yarn until it disappeared down a large hole in the ground. Still determined to retrieve it, he climbed into the pothole which soon opened out into a wider passage. He spotted a faint light filtering down and, with curiosity overcoming fear, he inched along the slimy floor with toads crawling around his feet and bats flitting overhead. The light grew brighter as he advanced until the passage suddenly opened out into a vast vaulted hall. A fire blazed in the centre without any apparent fuel and illuminated the walls of the cavern and its sleeping occupants. For there, sitting on golden thrones, were King Arthur and Queen Guinevere surrounded by their knights and some 30 couple of hounds. To one side was a table on which there was a sword, a garter and a bugle. Instinctively, the shepherd reached for the sword – it was the famous Excalibur – and drew it from its sheath. The moment he did so the eyes of everyone in the hall opened. Seemingly unperturbed by this, the shepherd then picked up the garter and cut it with the sword. This caused everyone to sit upright. At this point the shepherd's courage deserted him and he immediately slid Excalibur back into its scabbard, which sent everyone except Arthur back to sleep. The shepherd turned and ran out the way he had come, but as he did so Arthur was heard to intone:

> *O woe betide that evil day*
> *On which the witless wight was born*
> *Who drew the sword, the garter cut,*
> *But never blew the bugle horn.*

When the shepherd returned home, he told his story but could never remember how he found his way out of the cave or where exactly the entrance was. Perhaps the monotony of the clicking needles had lulled him into sleeping on the job; perhaps he had taken a little alcoholic refreshment; or perhaps King Arthur and his court still slumber in one of the many caverns that lie beneath Hadrian's Wall.

Another Arthurian legend surrounds two rocky outcrops known as King's Crag and Queen's Crag which stand north-east of Housesteads. The story goes that King Arthur was seated on a rock while talking to the queen, who was on the other rock combing out her long, black hair. She seemed more interested in her appearance than his conversation and so, annoyed at being ignored, he picked up a rock and threw it at her. With great dexterity she caught the rock on her comb and warded off the blow. The stone fell midway between them where it still lies with the mark of the comb upon it. The two crags lie about half a mile from each other and the stone probably weighs about 20 tons!

A short distance from the two crags lies Broomlee Lough where yet another legend tells of King Arthur's fabled treasure still lying at the bottom of the deep waters of the lake. It can only be drawn up by a blacksmith who is the seventh son of the seventh son of a blacksmith, and

OPPOSITE *Ghostly Roman soldiers still march along Hadrian's Wall, and King Arthur slumbers in an underground cavern.*

he has to forge an iron chain, cast one end into the lough and tie the other end to a team of pure white horses to drag the treasure from the water. The story goes that an attempt to recover the treasure was made many years ago. As directed, the blacksmith cast the chain into Broomlee Lough and in the centre of the lake he clearly saw a large wooden chest rise up to the surface. But suddenly a huge thunderstorm swept across Ridley Common and a torrential downpour soaked the blacksmith and his horses. At that moment the chain snapped and the chest disappeared back to the bottom of the lake. The blacksmith understood why when he looked at his team of horses. The rain had revealed the black nose of one of the 'white' horses which the dealer who had sold him the team had tried to cover up with whitewash.

Another hill close to Housesteads and the Wall is known as Cuddy's Crag, named, it is claimed, after St Cuthbert. Escaping from the Vikings who had destroyed their monastery on Holy Island, the monks of Lindisfarne took Cuthbert's corpse and searched for a new place to build a monastery. They might well have spent a night by the Wall, perhaps resting the saint's coffin on part of it, and this may be why the nearby hill became known as 'Cuddy's Crag' and why there is evidence that a small Christian church was established on the site.

Prudhoe Castle

NORTHUMBERLAND

Prudhoe, built in the 12th century on the site of an earlier fortification, is the third major castle along the River Tyne after Tynemouth and Newcastle. In the 19th century a Georgian manor house was built in the centre of the castle, replacing some of the medieval castle buildings and dividing the inner from the outer ward. There are many strange stories associated with the site. A white horse soundlessly paces the outer ward, and the sound of chanting has been heard coming from the chapel. A lady who lived in the East Tower and the manor house in the early 1950s had several unnerving experiences. One was the sound of a ball being bounced rhythmically up and down the steps – but there was never anyone there. She later discovered that, many years before, a young boy who became a priest had spent hours playing with a ball on the steps. On another occasion a couple living in the East Tower were woken by the sound of water being hurled at the door with great force. Yet another unexplained mystery was when the massive top of a vast oak table in the hall of the house was suddenly flung to the floor in the middle of the night. The noise it made shook the whole house and everyone thought that there had been a gas explosion. It took three men to put it back in position. Then there is the terrifying experience of a couple who used to live in the block, with their living room where the English Heritage shop now is. The husband had suffered with a type of facial paralysis but had been cured. One night he became aware that someone seemed to be prowling outside the living room window and bravely flung back the curtains to see who was there. As he did so a huge white shape hurtled towards him. Was it the White Horse of Prudhoe, a more sinister spectre or just a trick of the light? Whatever the reason, the unfortunate man found that his facial paralysis returned.

Hylton Castle

TYNE AND WEAR

A sad spectre in the form of a shivering, naked boy is reputed to haunt the 15th-century gatehouse tower that was once part of the impressive home of the Hylton family. The ghost is known as the 'Cauld Boy' and is said to be Robert Skelton, a young stableboy. He was caught sleeping instead of working by his master, Baron Robert de Hylton, who stabbed him to death with a pitchfork in a frenzy of rage. The body was thrown into the nearby lake, and the baron was granted a full pardon in 1609. That seemed to be that – until the troubled spirit of the murdered boy rose from his watery grave. His naked ghost was seen around the castle, usually in the kitchen, where he displayed a mischievous streak: if everything was neat and tidy, he would start to throw pots and pans about and generally cause mayhem; but if the kitchen was left in a mess, he very thoughtfully tidied it up. The Cauld Boy seems to have been a useful ghost to have around at times.

Taking pity on his nakedness, the kitchen staff one day decided to leave out a green hooded cloak by the fire. On the stroke of midnight, the ghost appeared and gratefully took away the cloak. However, he seems to have discarded it as he is still seen roaming naked around the site of Hylton Castle.

Today, the gatehouse can only be viewed from the outside. But you can still see the coats of arms of notable local families that adorn it – the Hyltons, Eures, Percys, Greys, Lumleys and Washingtons. The arms of the Washington family are 'on a field of argent, three mollets azure in chief, two bars gules' – three stars and two bars. It is said that George Washington adapted his family's coat of arms when he designed the Stars and Stripes flag of the United States.

Winter's Gibbet

NORTHUMBERLAND

The stark outline of a gibbet against a sombre sky is an eerie enough sight in itself, but this one has the added horror of what appears to be a human head dangling from it. The head is in fact carved out of wood and is all that now remains of an effigy of William Winter, the last man to be hung from a gibbet in England. In 1791 Winter, a gypsy with a history of crime, was arrested along with two female companions when an old lady called Margaret Crozier was found brutally murdered at her home at Raw Pele, just north of the village of Elsdon in the wild Northumbrian border country. Rumours had circulated about a secret hoard of money that Margaret had stashed away, the profits from her small drapery business, and the three accused admitted that they had robbed her but denied murder. However, on the evidence of an 11-year-old shepherd boy, they were all found guilty and hanged at Westgate, Newcastle. The bodies of the women were given to Surgeons' Hall to dissect but, in line with ancient custom, Winter's body was hung in chains from a gibbet close to the scene of his crime.

The gibbet, or 'stob' as it is called in Northumbria, was erected on Whiskershields Common and the body of William Winter remained there until it was picked clean by carrion. The gruesome sight no doubt added to Elsdon's rather inhospitable reputation at that time, celebrated in an old Northumbrian ballad:

Hae ye ivver been at Elsdon?
The world's unfinished neuk.
It stands amang the hungry hills
An' wears a frozen leuk.

The original gibbet was replaced in the late 19th century after the original decayed through time – and through the custom of people taking slivers from the gibbet to rub on their gums in the belief that it would cure the toothache! The wooden effigy was added as a reminder of Winter's fate – but it seems there is a less solid, supernatural reminder as well. The sound of skeletal bones rattling on the gibbet have often been heard on windy nights, and the shades of Winter and his companions have been spotted running from the scene of their crime.

OPPOSITE *Warkworth Castle,*
where the ghost of Harry
Hotspur peers out from an
upstairs window.

The legend of the Lambton Worm

Whist lads, haad yor gobs,
Aa'll tell ye aall an aafull story,
Whist lads, haad yor gobs,
An' aa'll tell ye 'bout the worm.

Celebrated in many a Northumberland ballad, this
folk tale tells how young John Lambton from Lambton Hall
near Durham went fishing one Sunday instead of going to
church. He stood on the banks of the River Wear for several
hours but all he caught was a black, tightly curled worm
with very sharp teeth. A passer-by warned John not to
throw it back in the river as it was a nasty creature that
would pollute the water. So he took it back home in his
basket and, not knowing what else to do with it, threw it
down the well (known forever after as Worm's Well). Over
the years John Lambton grew up – and so did the worm.

Unaware of the monster lurking in the depths of the
well, Lambton became a knight and went off to fight in
the Crusades. It was then that the worm, by now a vast
and vicious serpent, chose to emerge from the well to
satisfy its voracious appetite. To the horror of local people,
it started to eat sheep and cattle, and then developed a
taste for babies. There were several attempts to kill the
worm, but its razor-sharp fangs sliced through the
opposition. Finally the villagers had to resort to feeding
the Lambton Worm with the milk of hundreds of cows
in order to keep their families and flocks safe.

Seven years later, Sir John Lambton came back from
the Crusades and was horrified to see how his unusual
catch had developed. He took the advice of a wise woman
who told him that it was up to him to kill the worm as he
was the one who had brought it into the community. She
instructed him to go to the local blacksmith and get him
to make a suit of armour studded with sharp spear heads.
Wearing that armour, she predicted, he would vanquish
the Lambton Worm, but then he must kill the first living
creature that crossed his path or three times three
generations of Lambtons would be cursed to die
unnatural deaths.

Sir John did as the wise woman had told him, and
found the worm in its favourite place – curled round a
massive rock in the River Wear known as Worm's Rock.
It tried to wrap itself around him, but the spears on his
special armour cut it apart and the worm bled to death.
The victorious Sir John blew his horn to signal his success
and as a sign for his servants to let out his favourite hound,
which he intended to sacrifice to ensure no curse came
on his family. But everyone was so excited to be free of the
terrible worm that they forgot to let the dog out. Instead,
Sir John's father came rushing out to greet him. He couldn't
kill his father of course, and so the Lambton family had to
suffer the effects of the curse for nine generations.

Warkworth Castle

NORTHUMBERLAND

Mother and son spectres haunt this masterpiece of
medieval architecture, built by the Percy family who
wielded as much power as royalty in the 14th century.
The castle was designed both to reflect their importance
and as a means of keeping the troublesome border region
with Scotland under control. It is the ghost of Margaret
Neville, the wife of Henry de Percy, first Earl of
Northumberland, who is seen most often, a grey lady
drifting through the area between the Grey Mare's Tail
Tower and the west postern gate.

Her son, the famous Harry Hotspur, appears as a
face peering from the upstairs windows of the Duke's

Rooms in the main keep. Immortalised by Shakespeare in *Henry IV* and the subject of many a Northumberland ballad, Hotspur was killed at the Battle of Shrewsbury in 1403, but it seems that his spirit is loath to leave his ancestral home. He appeared on Halloween recently when there was a special event at the castle attended by several hundred people. Many of them reported seeing the ghostly face at the window – in rooms that are always kept locked.

There are eerie cold spots in the Grey Mare's Tail Tower and in one of the wine cellars – perhaps reflecting the days when these areas were used as prisons. The sufferings of those held here in barbaric conditions and cruelly tortured may have left their imprint in the atmosphere, and there is more solid evidence in the rough carvings made on some of the walls. One shows Christ and the twelve apostles in a touching portrayal of the carver's unswerving faith.

Tynemouth Priory and Castle

TYNE AND WEAR

Tynemouth's strategic headland has served as both a church and a fortress. Kings and saints were buried here, and the site has been an important defensive position against attacks from the Vikings in the 9th century, Scottish raiders in the 14th century, Napoleon in the 18th century and Germany in the 20th. With such a rich history, it is not surprising that a ghost still lingers here – a very old ghost who dates right back to the first Anglian monastery on the site. His name was Olaf and he was a Viking who took part in one of the frequent raids along the coast. Badly wounded in the battle, he was found by some of the monks who took him to the monastery and nursed him back to health. The charity of the monks was an inspiration to Olaf who took holy orders as soon as he was better and became a valued member of the religious community. Then the Vikings returned – and this time Olaf's brother was with them and was killed in the fierce fighting. Olaf was praying in the chapel when the news was brought to him, and his grief was so great that he died of a broken heart. Now his ghost haunts the coastline, always looking out to sea, and always on days when a brisk west wind blows across the North Sea from his homeland.

Brinkburn Priory

NORTHUMBERLAND

The borderlands were a dangerous place. Castles such as Warkworth could defend themselves and the immediate locality and so offered some deterrent against raiders and invaders, but other places were not so lucky. In the 14th century gangs of marauding Scots terrorised these regions, and soft targets such as Brinkburn Priory were at great risk. Founded in the 12th century for Augustinian canons, Brinkburn Priory had to trust to the power of God as its main defence, though it did have another form of defence – its position. Set in a deep valley and almost entirely surrounded by the River Coquet, which makes an extravagant meander at this point, the priory was set in an ancient forest. In summer its buildings were completely obscured by the leaves of the trees. Tradition has it that, on one occasion, a raiding party of Scots passed right by the priory, unable to spot even the top of a turret above the canopy of greenery. The monks had been warned that raiders were in the area and fully expected an imminent attack, but the day passed without incident. Overjoyed to have escaped, they prepared for a service of thanksgiving and rang the bells of the church. The Scots, unfortunately, were still not far away and the sound of the bells caused them to turn back, follow the noise and ransack the priory. The monks were so fed up with the bells that they cut them down and threw them into the river. The water close to the priory is known as Bell Pool and parts of a bell have been found on the other side of the river.

There is another explanation for the bells being cut down and thrown out of the priory church – the fairies. The magical setting of Brinkburn Abbey is so enchanting that you can quite believe the legend that fairies once lived here. These woods had apparently always been the home of the fairies of Northumbria, and they saw the spread of Christianity and the building of the priory as a threat. Determined to still the strident call to prayer of the priory's bells, the fairies fought back by magicking them off their ropes and into the river.

Perhaps the fairies were finally converted because the very last of the Northumberland fairies is reputedly buried in a tiny grave hidden in the abbey churchyard. Some

people say that this is because the priory eventually converted the local people to Christianity and so effectively killed the last of the fairies. But belief in the Little People remained strong throughout the country and was never completely quashed. Writing in the 17th century, Dr Corbet, the Bishop of Norwich, reported many sightings of the Little People – and in fact, even today, we still have a wistful longing for the magic of fairyland. Tinkerbell from J M Barrie's *Peter Pan*, Puck from Shakespeare's *A Midsummer Night's Dream* and the fairy on the Christmas tree still strike a chord.

ABOVE *Thomas, Earl of Lancaster, stalks the mystical ruins of Dunstanburgh Castle, carrying his severed head.*

Dunstanburgh Castle

NORTHUMBERLAND

The ruins of this medieval castle are straight out of a fairy story. It stands on a basalt crag above the sea, and its crumbling walls look like the jagged teeth of a mythical monster. But it was once the largest and most important castle in Northumberland and it still exudes power, majesty and the most awe-inspiring beauty. It was built by Thomas, Earl of Lancaster, who was one of the most powerful men in England in the early 14th century. He led the revolt of the barons against his uncle, King Edward II, and Edward's unpopular lover, Piers Gaveston, and Dunstanburgh was an ideal stronghold from which to launch the revolt. But the rebellion was quashed and Thomas was executed for treason in 1322. He suffered a grisly death. Either the blade of the axe was blunt or the executioner was not on form that day, because it took a total of eleven blows with the axe before Lancaster's head was finally severed from his body. Now his fearsome ghost wanders through the castle carrying the bloody head whose face is still contorted with the agony that he suffered centuries ago.

The cries of the gulls and the sea crashing on the rocks below are the usual sounds of Dunstanburgh, but every now and again the piercing notes of a horn cut through the air. This strange sound is reputed to be the horn blown by Sir Guy the Seeker. According to legend, Sir Guy was a wandering knight who happened to be riding near Dunstanburgh one day when he was caught in a thunderstorm. He took shelter under the arched entrance of the castle gatehouse and waited for the rain to ease. Suddenly a shrouded figure appeared and ordered Sir Guy to follow him. In true knightly fashion he didn't just gallop off as fast as his horse could carry him, but trustingly followed the spectral figure into the bowels of the castle to a secret room – one of the many hidden rooms that appear in legend time and time again throughout the country. At Dunstanburgh the subterranean prison housed a beautiful lady and a table on which lay a sword and a horn. Sir Guy was told that the lady would be free if he made the right choice between the sword and the horn. He made his choice immediately, and picked up the horn and blew it as hard as he could. No sooner had the last echoes of the horn faded than Sir Guy found himself back in the castle keep watching the rain. However, he was not a man to give up easily and he searched the castle tirelessly trying to find the entrance to the secret room. And apparently he is still looking – the figure of a knight has been seen stumbling through the ruins on an endless quest, while the keening notes of the horn are a constant reminder of his failure. Meanwhile, somewhere in Dunstanburgh Castle, the lovely lady still waits for someone to make the right choice and free her.

Chillingham Castle

NORTHUMBERLAND

There have been so many sightings of ghosts at this medieval castle near Alnwick that it can with justification claim to be the most haunted castle in Britain. The most famous apparition is the 'Radiant' or 'Blue' Boy who used to appear in the Pink Room on the stroke of midnight. The horrific cries of a child in an agony of pain and fear heralded the appearance of this spirit, seeming to come from a certain spot in the thick bedroom wall. As they faded, a bright glow started to form in the fireplace, growing in size until it eventually took the shape of a young boy dressed in a blue costume reminiscent of the style worn in the Restoration period. In the 1920s the wall out of which the Radiant Boy appeared was partly demolished, and the bones of a small boy, some blue fabric and the skeleton of a man were revealed. They were given a proper burial and from then on the Radiant Boy seems to have found peace. Every now and then, however, a guest sleeping in that room reports seeing blue flashes which are usually explained away as due to an electrical fault. The strange thing is that there are no electricity cables in the wall.

The ghost of an abandoned wife walks the castle in a fruitless search for her husband. Lady Mary Berkeley was the wife of Ford, Lord Grey of Wark and Chillingham and Earl of Tankerville, but he ran off with her sister, Lady Henrietta. Many people have heard the rustle of a silk dress sweeping the floor as she passes by, and felt an ice-cold draught. Another ghostly lady reputedly steps out of a portrait in the nursery, terrifying children and their nurse by following them around, and in the library disembodied voices hold an earnest conversation. Only the whispered intonation of the voices can be heard; the actual words cannot be made out and the sounds cease as soon as anyone tries to listen to what is being said.

Below stairs the ghost of a white lady has been seen in the inner pantry. This was the place where the family silver was stored, and so it was kept locked at night with a footman standing guard over it. One night the footman was confronted by a lady dressed in white who asked for a drink of water. Thinking it was one of the guests, he instinctively turned round to get a glass for her, but the lady had gone when he turned back. It was then that he realised in horror that he was locked in the room and only a ghost could have passed through the door. Later psychic investigations pointed to a lady who had suffered a long, slow death from poisoning and developed an unquenchable thirst for water.

There are even more ghosts outside, with a complete phantom funeral procession appearing in the Topiary Garden. It seems that this castle well deserves its reputation!

Lindisfarne Priory

NORTHUMBERLAND

Situated on Holy Island off the Northumberland coast, and linked to the mainland by a tidal causeway, Lindisfarne Priory has been a place of miracles and myths for over a thousand years. St Cuthbert led the monastic community here in the 7th century and it is not surprising to find his spirit still haunting the island that became one of the most important centres of Christianity in Anglo-Saxon England and remains a place of pilgrimage today. His ghost has often been seen in the Norman priory and by the rocks known as St Cuthbert's Beads. To give them their proper name, these are in fact fossil crinoid columnals, but legend claims that St Cuthbert actually makes them, sitting on one rock and using another as an anvil. The sound of hammering heard at night is attributed to the saint working

OPPOSITE *A statue of St Cuthbert, whose spirit still pervades Holy Island.*

away at making his giant rosary beads. Sir Walter Scott used this myth in his epic poem 'Marmion', describing how the nuns at Whitby Abbey were intrigued by the story:

> *But fain Saint Hilda's nuns would learn*
> *If on a rock, by Lindisfarne,*
> *St Cuthbert sits, and toils to frame*
> *The sea-borne beads that bear his name;*
> *Such tales had Whitby fishers told,*
> *And said they might his shape behold*
> *And hear his anvil sound:*
> *A deadening clang – a huge dim form,*
> *Seen but and heard when gathering storm*
> *And night were closing round.*

In what must be one of the earliest reported sightings of a ghost, St Cuthbert also apparently appeared to, and foretold the destiny of, none other than Alfred the Great!

A spectral procession of monks crosses the causeway at certain times, and a monk studiously reading from a parchment has been seen in the ruins. Another ghostly monk stands sentinel by the shore looking out to sea, only to disappear slowly into the sand. It is thought that he is keeping watch in case of attack as the island suffered relentless raids from the Vikings. Its isolation had made it a perfect place to found a religious community, but it also made it vulnerable. In AD 793 legends tell of whirlwinds and dragons appearing in the sky foretelling the destruction of the early monastery by the Danes. The monks fled, taking the miraculously undecayed body of St Cuthbert with them. They trekked across the north of England in search of a site to found a new community and finally ended their journey at the perfect spot – a rocky outcrop above the River Wear where St Cuthbert was laid to rest and where the monks laid the foundations of what would later become, under the Normans, the most beautiful cathedral in the world – in Durham.

OPPOSITE *The causeway to Holy Island is haunted by a spectral procession of monks.*

OVERLEAF *Statue,
Duncombe Park, Yorkshire.*

Life is a game that must be played:

This truth at least, good friend, we know;

So live and laugh, nor be dismayed

As one by one the phantoms go.

EDWARD ARLINGTON ROBINSON, 'BALLADE BY THE FIRE, CHILDREN OF THE NIGHT'